Castle Touring Guides

The Heart and West of Fife

Graham S. Coe

COECAST

Sancton

Castle Touring Guides
The Heart and West of Fife

First Published 1999
© Graham S. Coe 1999

Published by COECAST

Available through GOBLINSHEAD
130B Inveresk Road, Musselburgh , EH21 7AY, Scotland
Tel: 0131 665 2894   Fax: 0131 653 6566   Email: goblinshead@sol.co.uk

British Library Cataloguing in Publication Data
A catalogue record for this book is available from the British Library.

ISBN 1 899874 25 9

Castle Touring Guides

THE EAST NEUK OF FIFE
Published in October 1995 and covered the castles of St Andrews, Randerston, Balcomie, Crail, Airdrie, Isle of May, Pittarthie, Kellie, Newark, Ardross, Kilconquhar, Largo, Pitcruvie, Lundin, Aithernie, Struthers and Scotstarvit. The guide also encompassed St Andrews, Crail, Anstruther, Pittenweem, St Monans, Elie and Earlsferry and Ceres, while not forgetting where to eat, where to stay and where to go.

THE HOWE OF FIFE
Published in 1996 and covered the castles of Carslogie, Kilmaron, Lordscairnie, Parbroath, Collairnie, Fernie, Monimail, Denmylne, Ballinbreich, Creich, Mountquhanie, Naughton, Easter Kinnear, Kirkton, Earlshall, Cruivie, Pitcullo and Dairsie.

Planned for 2000
EDINBURGH & THE LOTHIANS - the first known complete photographic guide to all the fortified buildings in the region.

Castle Touring Guides

The Heart and West of Fife

Contents

About the Author

I have always had a general interest in castles, but until 1990 it was directed towards the significant buildings in the care of the national conservation bodies.

While on holiday that year, I bought Mike Salter's *Discovering Scottish Castles*, which listed over 1000 castles regardless of structural state.

A touring holiday the following year started the lengthy objective of photographing all of them. For every well known / well visited castle there seemed to be 20 others which were passed on a daily basis without anyone recognising their existence. Each of them concealed centuries of history.

Having been a devotee of Scottish holidays since 1981, it seemed natural to combine the two passions. What started as a hobby quickly developed into an opportunity to promote all castles and also raise the profile of other tourist attractions.

At the launch of my first guide at Fernie Castle, I overheard the Laird of Balgonie and Eddergoll trying to encourage fellow castle owners to form an organisation – but none of them had the time. I wrote to the Laird offering help, and subsequently conducted a mail-shot to all "occupied" properties. Some 70 responded, but not all of them positively. Nevertheless an inaugural meeting did take place at Culcreuch Castle in June 1996. (More details of the Scottish Castles Association can be found on pages 83-4).

I was born in Rotherham, educated at Maltby Grammar School and spent the first 23 years of my working life at British Steel. Starting as a Commercial Apprentice, my first attachment was in the Statistics Department. I then moved to the Hollerith Section which was an early computer installation. There was an opportunity to go on a programming course (1963), and the rest as they say is history. My British Steel career was always centred in the Rotherham area, and it covered all of the technical and management roles. In 1984 the family (wife Janet and our three children Paul, Neil and Michael) moved close to York, buying a village Post Office and Corner Shop. I changed career direction, into Local Government, but remained in the computer field.

Progression took me from Selby District Council to Boothferry Borough Council (Goole) and then to Stockton-on-Tees Borough Council, where I was appointed as Information Technology Manager in 1991. Having taken the Council through the Local Government Review of 1996, when Stockton became a unitary authority delivering all local services, I then joined Ultracomp Ltd as a Principal Consultant covering all Information Technology and Local Government issues.

Returning to the initial objective of photographing all the castles of Scotland, it has been important to try and establish how many there are by amalgamating all know references. The recent *The Castles of Scotland* by Martin Coventry has become the definitive catalogue of the fortified buildings and sites. Currently there appears to be around 1420 which have at least some masonry to see. My total has just passed the 500 mark, and requires some effort to locate and get permission to photograph where appropriate.

It is the intention of this guide and all future guides to be accurate in all respects. If you find any mistakes, inaccuracies, oversights or additional material worthy of inclusion, then it will help future publications. Send your suggestions to:

Mr G S Coe
c/o Goblinshead
130B Inveresk Road
Musselburgh EH21 7AY
Scotland

The Heart
of Fife

The West
of Fife

Acknowlegements

The FRONT COVER is Balgonie Castle and the REAR COVER is Pitcairlie.

There have been significant contributions to the construction of this guide book, those whose knowledge has been fully utilised:

- **Stuart Morris of Balgonie yr** (information on Balgonie Castle, Leslie House and Balfour House)
- **Eddy Wilson** (information on Balfour House, Grange, Couston Castle)
- **Martin Coventry** (Goblinshead) who takes credit for the design and preparation of the guide, and without whose assistance it would not have been possible

FOR PERMISSION TO PHOTO-GRAPH AND/OR PUBLISH

- **J G Burgess** (Falkland Palace)
- **The National Trust for Scotland** (Falkland Palace and Culross)
- **Robert Balfour of the Balbirnie Estate** (Pitillock House)
- **Historic Scotland** (Ravenscraig Castle and Commendator's House, Inchcolm)
- **Iain Maciver** (Strathendry Castle)
- **Bill and Muriel McLay** (Pitcairlie including photographs and information)
- **J Pringle** (internal shots of Pitcairlie)
- **Mr & Mrs Inglis** (Fordell Castle)
- **Craig Lindsay** (Pitreavie Castle including information)
- **Dr Jack R.F. Burt/Dunfermline Heritage Trust** (Abbot House)
- **Stuart Fisher** (Dunimarle Castle)
- **The caretaker at Tulliallan Castle**
- **Mr A Fraser/Factor** (Balmuto Tower)
- **Mary A Patterson** (Knockdavie Castle)
- **Mrs White** (Myres Castle)
- **Nicholson Street Guides** (street plans)

FOR INFORMATION, HISTORY, AND BACKGROUND

Royal Commission on the Ancient and Historical Monuments of Scotland (Inventory of Monuments in Fife, Kinross and Clackmannan), and black and white drawings of Maiden Castle, Fordell Castle, Inchcolm Abbey, Pitreavie Castle, Hill House, Tulliallan Castle and Knockdavie Castle)

The publishers are taking every step to try to secure permission to reproduce copyright works but in the event of any omissions they will be pleased to make any amends at the earliest opportunity. This reflects the change in copyright, in 1996, to extend it to 70 years after the authors death. The two titles affected are:

- Fife Pictorial and Historical
- Domestic and Castellated Architecture of Scotland

Introduction

Fife is a peninsula, some 20 Kilometres wide, sandwiched between the Firths of Forth and Tay, and has a unique combination of history, a rich collection of historic buildings and natural beauty. Above all, visitors will quickly recognise the friendliness of the "Fifers".

The Kingdom of Fife is so called because Dunfermline was the home of Scotland's kings from the days of Malcolm III, in the 11th century, until the Union of the Crowns of Scotland and England under James VI in 1603.

This guide covers two arbitrary areas, which for simplicity have been defined as the Heart of Fife and West Fife. The Heart is a slice of the Kingdom roughly between Newburgh and Leven as the eastern extremity, and Kinghorn and Loch Ore in the west.

There is a stark contrast between the tranquil rural northern section to the Tay coastline, and the busy southern border with the Firth of Forth, but equally they both have their attractions.

It is the third in a series covering the Kingdom, which in total concentrates on over 70 castles. In the Heart they range from the historical focus of Falkland Palace and Ravenscaig in the care of The National Trust for Scotland and Historic Scotland respectively, to the equally intriguing but commercially different Balgonie and Pitcairlie. Additionally it is full of interest with the imposing but secluded structures of Strathendry and Wemyss, while on the other hand there are the crumbling remains of Hallyards.

The circular tour starts in the small town of Falkland, full of picturesque old houses and cobbled streets, and moves southwards passing the contrastingly different new town of Glenrothes, then to the coast at Leven, one of Fife's most popular resorts.

Travelling down the coast you will pass through Buckhaven, and then step back in time by visiting the villages of East and West Wemyss, and the ancient town of Dysart, which is not to be missed, before arriving at the main shopping centre of Fife - Kirkcaldy. The pleasant setting of Kinghorn is the furthest point south on the trail, before heading back northwards to finish near Auchtermuchty.

West Fife has a similar diversity of rolling countryside and active town centres. Historic Scotland has a presence with the 11th century Aberdour Castle, and Dunfermline Palace, while The National Trust for Scotland oversees Culross Palace. For sheer magnificence Fordell Castle and Tulliallan Castle should not be missed.

Touring the West, it starts in Aberdour and for some time hugs the coastline, briefly interrupted by a visit to six sites in and around Dunfermline, the birthplace of Andrew Carnegie.

Through the historically interesting Culross, the journey loops back at the western tip of the Kingdom and the Tulliallan stronghold and meanders to finish in Burntisland.

While some of the castles in the guide are open to the public and therefore details of access arrangements are included, the majority are on private land and can only be seen from a distance. Under no circumstances should they be visited without obtaining permission from the owners/occupiers.

Many castles are in a dangerous state and visitors should take extreme care before entering the building, even having sought the owners permission.

How to Use This Guide

Please read the guide thoroughly so that, before you move on to the next castle, you spend time exploring the towns and villages described in some detail in the additional information section near the end of this guide.

The route is always circular (clockwise), which means that you can join it at any point and make a complete tour round if you wish. At the point of entry look at the castle in which you are interested and refer to the directions in a shaded box near the top of the page.

Other places of interest en route are linked to the additional information section within the "directions" instructions. To help the weary traveller overcome the frustration of not knowing where to stop for refreshments, there are inns, public houses, restaurants, bed and breakfast, and hotels listed.

Towns and villages which are worthy of further exploration are covered in some detail but it is suggested that fuller information should be sought from Tourist Information Centres, details of which are included in the guide.

Please check opening times of any tourist attraction, especially out of season. They do vary.

Do not forget your camera, a pair of binoculars, and Ordnance Survey Maps (Nos 58, 59, 65 and 66).

Having said all that do not miss the scenery.

Castle Touring Guides

The Heart of Fife

Map 1 - The Heart of Fife

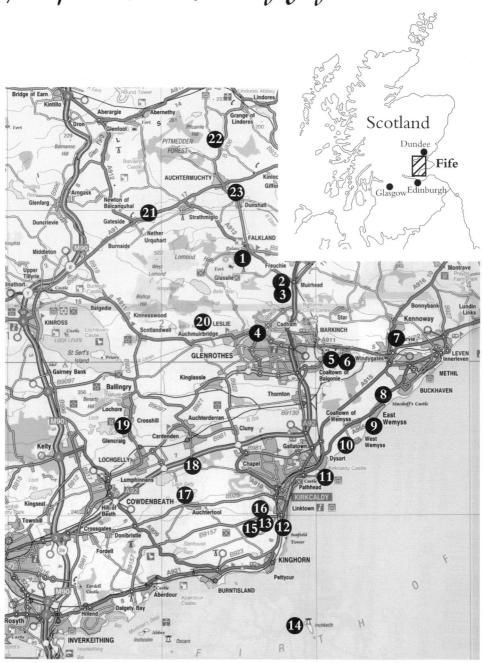

© Crown copyright 1999

1 Falkland Palace

Ordnance Survey (OSR) = NO 254075

Falkland Palace

a great quadrangular structure, of which the buildings now standing formed a part, was begun on the area previously occupied by the steading. The old castle was gradually abandoned, as the new work neared completion (1541).

Today only the south range and the gatehouse are complete. In 1840 these underwent a restoration followed by an even more extensive restoration 50 years later by the 3rd Marquis of Bute, who became Hereditary Constable, Captain and Keeper of the Palace in 1887. He completely restored the south range and made it habitable again. He also undertook extensive research, tracing the foundations of the old castle and consolidating what remains of the ruined east range. His architect was John Kinross.

There is a notable building in the low ground to the north, which was possibly built in 1531-2. Attached to it is probably the only

Structure

Hunting-palace of the Stuart dynasty, it was perhaps more of a royal home than a place of State. Its architecture is majestic, and its south range is the finest work of its period in Scotland.

Foundations of an early castle remain exposed as a result of a series of excavations. They evidently represent what is referred to as the "Tower of Falkland" in 1337, when it was levelled to the ground by English invaders. It must have been replaced before 1401.

Repairs and additions continued in the 15th century, and in the second half its housing accommodation was much extended. About 1530 a new phase opened, when

Chapel Royal, Falkland Palace

example of the kind in Scotland, the tennis court begun in 1538. It is an oblong enclosure with timber penthouses on two sides.

The visitor enters by way of the East Port, and from there it leads through the remains of the outer wall of the east range into the cellar passages of the palace. A turnpike stair leads up a few steps to the courtyard.

The South Range is in the best state of preservation, and this range was already standing when James IV rode away to his death at Flodden. It contains the Chapel Royal, with the Captain's quarters in the Gatehouse.

The roofless East Range is about the same age as the South Range, and an interesting feature is a cross-house which projects eastwards form the building line on the opposite side to the courtyard. The East Range contained the Royal Apartments.

The ruined North Range is marked only by the outline remains of its foundations, now the site of the rose garden. This was the oldest part of the palace, built by James II. Prior to the East Range here was the Great Hall where they held Council. It was burnt in 1654 when occupied by a garrison of Cromwell's troops who were occupying Fife and the rest of Scotland.

History

The castle and lordship of Falkland belonged in the fourteenth century to the Earls of Fife, and in 1371 were in the hands of Robert Stewart, Earl of Fife and Menteith, son of Robert II. Under the title of Duke of Albany, that Earl was Regent of Scotland, and occupied the castle of Falkland as his residence for thirty four years. It was then that the title of Palace was given to this residence; but the palace which then existed has been entirely removed, and it is doubtful whether the existing building is even on the site of the old one.

It was in this old palace that David, Duke of Rothesay, was imprisoned by his uncle Robert Stewart, Duke of Albany, and where he died, under suspicious circumstances, in 1402.

When James I returned from his captivity in 1424, Murdo, Duke of Albany, the son and successor of Duke Robert, was executed, and Falkland was annexed to the Crown. The domain is pleasantly situated in the valley of the Eden, and hence it became a favourite retreat for the Scottish kings. The three first Jameses often resorted to it, and the town of Falkland was erected into a royal burgh by James II in 1458. James III and James IV

Falkland Palace

Falkland – Interior of Courtyard (c. 1892)

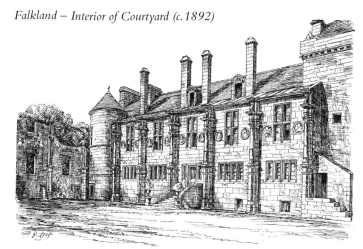

occasion was the quincentenary of the granting of the Royal Charter to the burgh by James II. After being received at the Town Hall the present Queen and Prince Philip watched a performance of a masque re-enacting that event.

The National Trust for Scotland assumed responsibility for the building in 1952.

are both said to have carried on works at the palace, and from the style of the south front it belongs to the latter half of the fifteenth century.

The interior of the existing building fronting the courtyard was added by James V, who was particularly attached to this residence. It was from here he escaped out of the hands of the Earl of Angus in 1528, and here he died, in 1542, broken-hearted at the rout of Solway Moss.

After James's death Mary of Guise often lived at Falkland, and Queen Mary was fond of retiring to it as a hunting-seat.

James VI resided much here for his favourite pastime of the chase, and to judge from the style of what remains, he seems to have added considerably to the size of the building.

The palace was occupied both by Charles I and Charles II. After the battle of Sheriffmuir, in 1715, it became the abode for a short period of a very different sort of person. Rob Roy Macgregor took possession of it, harried the country around, and carried off much booty to the Highlands.

In Charles II's time the building was greatly injured by fire.

In 1958, over 300 years after Charles II, the last king to live in the palace, had left it, a reigning sovereign visited Falkland. The

Extensive gardens, Visitor Centre, shop.
Disabled access to the gardens.
Open April to October.
Tel: 01337 857397.

Royal Burgh of Falkland

Before moving on you should spend time exploring this exquisite Royal Burgh. Details can be found on page 73 towards the back of this guide.

Bruce Fountain, Falkland

2 *Pitillock House*

Ordnance Survey (OSR) = NO 278052

Leave Falkland down the High Street/
East Port to the junction. Turn right on
the A912. After 3.7 Km (2.3 miles) turn
right into an unmarked lane (2 right turns
beyond the East Lomond View Point
turn). In a matter of a few metres you
enter the farm area, and Pitillock House
is on your left.

'Conland Castle'

Structure

Incorporates a 16th century L-plan tower
house, which was remodelled about the 1850s
in a classical style.

History

Pitillock was possessed by Mr Balfour and
appeared in a charter of David II, under the
name Peteclach, having then been resigned
by Duncan, Earl of Fife, and confirmed by

Pitillock House

the King to Christian Bruce. The Lumsdaines
held it till 1651, when it was acquired by
Baillie of Falkland, and passed from him to
the Balfours of Balbirnie.

There remains a mystery in this area, which
has been detailed in "Fife : Pictorial and
Historical" under the name of Conland
Castle.

The barony of Condeland, renamed
Conland, was in the possession of the
Lumsdaines in the 15th century. It came by
succession to James Lumsdaine of Drums in
1507, and he obtained a charter uniting his
two estates into the free barony of Condeland.
In the same year he disposed of
Condeland to Sir David
Murray, son of Sir Andrew
Murray and of Margaret
Barclay; and Sir David
reconstituted his Fifeshire
possessions, uniting
Condeland, Pitillock, and
Gospetry to the barony of
Arngask. Conland remained in
the hands of the Murrays until
1590, at which time it became
the property of Andrew
Lundie, who added to it the
lands of Powrane, which had
belonged to the Lumsdaines of
Airdrie from 1450 till that time. The estate of
Conland was afterwards divided into Easter
and Wester Conland, the former being in the
possession of John Balfour and the latter in
the hands of William Yeaman.

3 Bandon Tower

Ordnance Survey (OSR) = NO 277043

Bandon Tower about 1875

> Continue along the track for another 1.5 Km (1 mile) and the ruined tower stands in the middle of a field on your left.

Structure

It consists of a rectangular tower with a plain square keep, of the 16th century, but the whole structure is very much broken down. In height there have been three floors and an attic each containing a single chamber. The ground floor has probably been vaulted, but it has fallen. Three of the walls have mostly gone, but the masonry is of rubble, roughly coursed with dressings of quoins at openings. The remains of a large fireplace exist in the south-east end, with a what used to be a newel stair.

Brief History

In 1498 Alan Balfour of Bandon ("Ballindone") conveyed the estate to his eldest son, Duncan. It is said that it belonged at one time to a branch of the Bethune family, but that must be either have been very early or very late in its history. David Balfour of "Banedone" is among the witnesses to a charter of 1580. In 1630, Michael Balfour of Bandon succeeded his father David, and it is possible that it was afterwards held by a Bethune.

Bandon Tower

4 Leslie House

Ordnance Survey (OSR) = NO 259019

Continue on the minor road for 1.1 Km (0.7 miles) to the main road. Turn left on the A92 to the roundabout and return on the A92. Turn right on the B969 (Leslie) after 3.4 Km (2.1 miles). Straight across the two roundabouts (Coul and Pitcoudie), and then turn right at the third (Leslie), where Fettykil Fox is on the left. From the Leslie roundabout drive for 1 Km (0.6 miles) and the entrance is the left turn just before the Greenside Hotel.

Any visitor approaching Leslie House from the town of Leslie is met by a most magnificent view of the house. As the drive, banked by trees and bushes, widens out it is edged with more formal lawns planted with the most majestic trees. They are a natural frame for this view of the building. Above the front entrance is the coat of arms of the Leslie family and their motto "Grip Fast". How this crest came into being is a good place to start the story of Leslie House.

Structure

The original "palace" of Leslie, which was built round a quadrangle immediately east of the town of Leslie, was destroyed by fire in 1763, but the west wing was reconstructed in 1767 by John, Earl of Rothes, to form the present mansion.

So far as the walls are concerned, the earlier work can be traced only on the east side, where it extends to a height of two storeys. On the north, partly incorporated in the present building and partly extending eastward beyond it, is a vaulted ground floor of store-houses and kitchens which survived the fire.

History

Batholemew de Leslyn was an exiled Hungarian knight who was at the Flemish court with Princess Margaret (later to become Queen Margaret of Scotland). He was charged to bring the princess, her brother and sister, safely to Scotland. As no safe route could be found through England they made passage by ship and landed safely at Queen's Hope, Queensferry. After Margaret married the King, Malcolm Canmore, Bartholemew was made her chancellor and when travelling she rode behind him, a special pad having been added to his saddle for her comfort. The story goes that on one occasion that they had to ford a river in spate, Bartholemew reached behind to hold her and told her to "Grip Fast" or hold tight to his belt. She replied "Gin the buckle bide" meaning that she hoped the buckle would hold. Thereafter two gold buckles were gifted to him as a token of gratitude and thereby lies the tale of the three buckles on the coat of arms and the motto. Bartholemew settled in the district of Garioch in Aberdeenshire in the reign of William I. From his descendants came the branch of the family who built Leslie House.

Records show that as long ago as the middle of the 12th century a dwelling place stood on this site and was known as the Palace of Leslie and was described as being "set amidst a forest of trees".

Having won favour in high places, George Leslie of Rothes was in 1457 elevated to the peerage of Scotland and was created first Earl of Rothes. It is recorded that at that time he created the Barony of Leslie, and this was later ratified by his great grand-children who granted a new charter to the inhabitants of the town which gave the people much more freedom. During this period the family became the power behind the throne of Scotland and at the height of their prosperity it was said they could ride from the shores of the Firth of Forth to the shores of the Moray Firth without ever leaving their own ground.

The family have a colourful history. The 4th Earl, George, was accused of aiding his sons Norman (Master of Leslie) and Patrick (Master of Lindores) in the murder of Cardinal Beaton. He was acquitted of this charge although both his sons were involved along with others and indeed the dagger used is supposedly still in the family's possession.

John 6th Earl of Rothes carried the Sword of State when Charles II was crowned at Scone in 1651. It was he who around 1660 built on this site a magnificent mansion similar in style to Holyrood Palace. It was built four square with a centre courtyard. The building contained 80 bedrooms, excluding dressing rooms and other apartments. The picture gallery was reputedly even longer than that in Holyrood.

Disaster struck on Christmas Day 1763 when a large party was in residence for the festivities on Christmas Eve. Venison was being roasted over the fire in the hall and also the coachmen were melting wax for the carriage lamps. After dinner the smell of burning was detected and a search was carried out to find the source but nothing untoward was found. Satisfied the Earl continued with his party. During the night a guest, young General Dalrymple, was awakened by a choking smell of smoke and found the wall of his bedroom on fire. The entire mansion was burnt to the ground. It was a night of wind and snow so thick that the townspeople, who were attracted to the scene and attempted to help, were hidden

Leslie House

from each other as they tried to fetch water. As the storm raged the wind fanned the blaze so that the sky was lightened by its brilliance. A newspaper report of the time describes how the Earl could be seen silhouetted by the blaze with his military cape swirling around his shoulders directing the evacuation of the building. This he did so skilfully that no lives were lost and many of the paintings, books and other treasures were saved.

The ruins smouldered on for several days and it was believed that the fire had indeed started in the fireplace by a beam becoming scorched and then bursting into flame when fanned by a draught.

Following the fire the Earl stayed in Edinburgh until he had gathered enough money to rebuild. This took him 3 years and it was in 1766 that Leslie House as it is today was built on the site of the west wing of the former mansion. Stones from the ruins were used to build the terraced gardens on the south side of the house overlooking the river Leven. On the back of the present house evidence of the original stonework can also be seen.

Originally the South wing of the top floor was the Night Nursery and on the same floor a magnificent ballroom boasting the most beautiful crystal chandeliers was situated between the two staircases and ran the full width of the house.

On the first floor was the Countesses Boudoir (which is now the flat for the Officer in Charge) and the family drawing room with a wonderful view up the drive.

On the ground floor the layout remains almost unchanged with the dining room, kitchen and pantries, and the drawing room overlooking the River Leven. An interesting feature is the double door leading from the dining room and the lounge into what was the billiard room. They were presumably installed in order to deaden the sounds of the gentlemen at play.

The house remained in the possession of the Rothes family until 1919 when it was sold to a Major Crandell from London, who never lived in the house. He retained it for a few months and then sold it to Sir Robert Spencer Nairn. As Sir Robert saw the new town of Glenrothes encroaching he met with the Rev D P Thomson, who was on an evangelical mission in the area at that opportune time, and following their meeting he approached the Church of Scotland and offered Leslie House to them for use as an Eventide Home. This offer was gratefully received and Leslie House was opened on 8th June 1956 as a home for the elderly.

It seems fitting that the thread of Christianity should run throughout this proud history, from Queen Margaret of Scotland to Henrietta Countess of Rothes who started the first Sunday School in Leslie, actually within the house, and Leslie itself now being in the care of the Church of Scotland itself.

5 Balgonie Castle

Ordnance Survey (OSR) = NO 313007

Emerging from Leslie House drive, turn right on the A911 and follow the signs through a series of roundabouts towards Leven. After 5 Km (3.2 miles) turn right on the B9130 (Coaltown of Balgonie) which is situated just beyond the two bridges. Turn left at the next junction and after another 0.8 Km (0.5 miles) there is a left turn signposted Balgonie Castle, which is a further 0.8 Km on your left.

Introduction

On 19th August 1996 I stayed overnight at Balgonie Castle. It was not the first time in the castle, nor was it the first time I had met the Laird and his family, so there was no reason to be surprised. Wrong ! You have to see the scale of the task in hand to appreciate that this family is something special. They have to be special because their enthusiasm never wanes as they set about another day towards the ultimate objective of bringing Balgonie back to its original state, or as near to that as is possible. When that happens then it will be a truly great castle.

It would be acceptable if they took the easy way out and called it a day, but having taken a walk around their achievements to-date, you appreciate the progress that has been made. The Chapel and the Great Hall are a testament to their endeavours, attention to detail and

proof of their vast knowledge, not only of Balgonie but castles and their environment in general. The Laird is a self proclaimed "castle nut", and if truth be known it also applies to son Stuart and wife Margaret.

The formation of a Scottish Castles Association (details at the back of the guide) addressing the requirements of the many owners and supporters of the country's castles was muted in 1996. There is need to guess which family were at the forefront, with the author, in the initiation of the organisation.

To fully understand the magnitude, it all has been self financing with not one penny in grants. Remember that this a 14th century castle, and therefore it should have attracted substantial assistance from national and international bodies.

It is strongly recommended that you make the effort and visit. It is a real castle, a real home and with real people, with whom you will relate. Your guided tour has that personal touch.

Structure

Balgonie is a courtyard castle. The oldest part is the main tower, built around 1360. It is a typical example of an early Scottish tower

Balgonie Castle

Chapel, Balgonie

floor contains three rooms, the first being the 1496 kitchen. In the vault above the fire are signs of what would have been a 15th century dumb-waiter. The original use of the second room is unknown, but through this room is the 14th chapel. The first floor was entered by a re-

house, being of five floors, with a room per floor, and all under a parapeted roof. The tower was originally entered by a wooden staircase to the first floor. The vaulted ground floor was entered from the first floor by means of a ladder. This room was used to store food, hence the presence of the ventilation slits in each wall. The vaulted first floor was the original great hall and still retains its window seats, which were removed from the other floors in the 17th century.

The unusual feature is the lack of a fireplace. The original fire was in the centre of the floor, with the smoke eventually entering two smoke vents housed in the gable walls. The second floor, or Laird's hall, was reached by a turnpike stair rising within the thickness of the wall. The fire-place in the north wall is almost seven feet wide and next to this is a garderobe which overhangs the outer wall.

The north range was added in 1496, incorporating 14th century corner towers, and the date of this wing can be accurately dated because in this year James IV visited Balgonie. He was so impressed by the mason's work, he gave them fourteen shillings. The style of this building is known as a Hall House - a castle in its own right. The vaulted ground

movable staircase, and the floor contains only two rooms - one being the main hall and the other would have been the Laird's private chamber. A further storey was added by the first Earl of Leven in the mid 17th century. The ten feet gap between the tower and the north range was filled in with a scale and platt tower (a 'straight' stair with landings) in 1666.

The east range dates from two distinct periods. The southern hall dates from the 15/16th century and was restored during the mid 17th century. The northern hall was built in 1702 for the 3rd Earl of Leven. The other two sides of the courtyard are enclosed by a barmkin wall. In the south-west corner is the gatehouse and on either side of the gate are two guard rooms. The northern one house a 15th century prison.

Balgonie illustrates the changing attitudes to habitation and defence over a period of 400 years, beginning with the needs for defence in the 14th century and ending with the demands for greater space and comfort in the 18th century - attitudes that have been influenced by times of war and peace, together with a greater awareness of architectural developments in other countries. Methods of construction can be detected by carefully studying the castle walls.

Within the tower are three models which depict different stages of the castle's development.

To the north of the castle is a wildlife garden which is available for studies of natural history.

History

The probable builder of the castle was Sir Thomas Sibbald of Balgonie, who witnessed a charter in 1371. His grandson, Sir Andrew, was Sheriff of Fife. Sir Andrew's daughter, Helen, married Sir Robert Lundin, Lord High Treasurer of Scotland, son of Sir John Lundin of the ilk and their son, Sir Andrew was also Sheriff of Fife. The Lundins retained possession of Balgonie until 1627, when the estate was sold to two sons of Sir John Boswell of Balmuto. However, they soon became bankrupt, and the estate was sold by their creditors in 1635, to the castle's most prominent Laird, Sir Alexander Leslie.

Leslie was born in Balvenie Castle, Banffshire, around 1580, the son of George Leslie, Captain of Blair Castle and Bailiff of Atholl. Shortly after 1600 he joined the Scots Brigade, in the Dutch service, in their war against Spain. In 1608 he was given a commission in the Swedish Army by King Gustavus Adolphus. In 1638 after a career spanning thirty years, in which he is said to have never lost a battle, he retired. Leslie has held many positions of authority, including Governor of the Southern Baltic. He had been knighted by the King and was created a German Count twice, but his greatest achievement was probably becoming the only foreigner to become Field Marshal of Sweden.

Leslie returned to Scotland, and Balgonie, at a time of great political and religious turmoil. Charles I was attempting to impose the "Rule of the Bishops" on his northern Kingdom. The solemn League of the Covenant was created to counteract this threat to the Scottish nation. The League raised an army with Leslie as its commander or Lord General. He bought Balgonie in 1635, and did most of his restoration in the next three years. In March 1639 Leslie laid siege to Edinburgh Castle, taking it in half an hour without losing a single man. The Army marched on the Borders to confront the King, and this confrontation was the basis of the satirical poem "There Was a Crooked Man". In retaliation, the King put a price of £500 on Leslie's head. A few months later the King made him a member of the Scottish Privy Council, and in 1641 he elevated Leslie to the peerage and

Great Hall, Balgonie

1st Earl of Leven and Lord Balgonie. It was David, 3rd Earl of Leven (who also inherited the Earldom of Melville) who raised the regiment that is now The King's Own Scottish Borderers. Leslie went on to command the Scottish Army during the English Civil War. After an eventful life he died of old age in his own bed, in Balgonie, on 4th of April 1661.

Balgonie – Plans

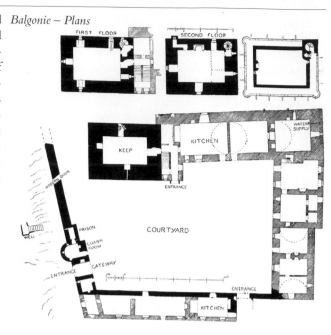

Contrary to popular belief, Balgonie was not destroyed by Rob Roy MacGregor. However in January 1716, while Rob Roy was ransacking Falkland, General Cadogan was marching his army to garrison the castle. On hearing of this, Rob Roy marched on Balgonie with 200 clansmen. On his way he had a skirmish at Markinch, where he took some Hanoverian prisoners.

The 3rd Earl was in Edinburgh at the time so there were only servants at Balgonie, who probably took one look at them and fled. The length of his stay is not recorded, it was unlikely to have been more than a week. The 8th Earl sold Balgonie in 1824 to Sir James Balfour of Whittinghame (grandfather of A J Balfour, 1st Earl of Balfour, Prime Minister 1902-5) who gave the estate to his second son Charles. By the 1840s letters were appearing in the Edinburgh press, concerned about the appalling state of Balgonie. Roofing was removed to avoid paying the Roof Tax.

The Balfour's turned the 350 acre Park into fields, with a coal mine at one end. The 5, or so, mile long wall still stands, together with the walls of the 11 acre walled garden. Following the heavy vandalism of the 1960s, the estate sold the castle to David Maxwell from Edinburgh in 1971. He carried out restoration to the tower. He sold the north and east wings to the then Fife County Council, who planned to transform them in to a museum and educational facilities. After being on the market for 4 or 5 years, it was bought by the Morris family, the current owners, in 1985. Raymond Morris became the 30th Laird of Balgonie, and the family was the first to live in the castle since 1824

The Ghosts of Balgonie

There has never been any attempt to dramatise or capitalise upon the presence of ghosts, quite the contrary: it is a matter of fact issue. The best known spectre is "Green Jeannie", and her appearances have been the subject of local discussion for over two hundred years. All the Laird's family have seen her, with the same description as pea-green in colour and having a long full-skirted dress and a hood which hides her face. Although not seen since 1994, her favourite haunt was in the ruinous

18th century wing.

The Great Hall is, however, the most haunted room, where inexplicably a skeleton was found under the floor in 1912 when the concrete floor was being laid. Voices are often heard, but are silent on entry. Occasionally there is a smell of pipe smoke. In 1996 Stuart saw a black figure of a man run in front of him towards the window, in what appeared to be medieval dress, and in 1997 he saw an apparition of a man's head drift out of the same room. It was wearing a collar and was suspended at head height.

A female waitress was setting up for a banquet, and felt someone brush past her back, but she was alone - this is the only physical contact.

The Laird's Hall has witnessed other sightings. The Lady of Balgonie woke from a snooze one winter evening in 1996 to see a grey figure like a statue standing in front of her. She said that he had a full lace collar, lace cuffs, slashed sleeves, long hair and a little goatee beard. There was enough time to look him up and down before he disappeared. It is believed to be the Earl of Leven.

In 1996 the Laird saw a grey figure of a man walk across the courtyard and hold out his hand as if he was opening a door. Months later a labourer who had worked at Balgonie in the 60s and 70s, said that he had seen the same figure at the same spot.

The Wedding Success

If you are considering a wedding with a difference, then this is the place to be. Although not an exhaustive list, couples have come from Scotland, England, France, Norway, Korea, Finland, USA, Australia, New Zealand, Poland, Malaysia, Germany and Hungary. To add to the list there is scheduled in 1999 a Chinese marriage. Always expect the unexpected. In June 1998 Lyndal Rhodes married Alistair Blades at Balgonie. At home in Brisbane, Lyndal found Balgonie on the internet, flew half way around the world, and then to

Wedding, Balgonie

be given away by the Laird. In December 1998 Lesley Ann Williams and fiance Mark Manktelow landed in the grounds by helicopter from Kent, and became the 410th couple to marry at the castle.

Balgonie is open to the public all year round, 10 a.m to 5 p.m., and there is a small entry charge for the guided tour by the Laird, Raymond S Morris of Balgonie & Eddergoll, or his son, Stuart.
The Chapel is available for Weddings and Christenings, while the Great Hall is available for receptions, recitals, parties, banquets etc. Tel: 01592 750119

6 Balfour House

Ordnance Survey (OSR) = NO 324003

Continue on the minor for 2 Km (0.5 miles) to the junction on the incline. Turn right, signed A911 to Windygates, through Milton of Coaltown for 300 metres (0.2 miles). At the end of the village turn right at the bus shelter, go over the bridge and take the left fork on the track. Park at the gate and walk across the field to the ruins.

Structure

It was developed from a late 16th century house with an extension of a century later. It was a L-shaped on plan, the main block facing south and the wing projecting northward in alignment with the old west gable. The wing contained a newel stair serving three floors. The lowest flight had been altered in the 17th century.

The original entrance lay not in the re-entrant angle but in the west wall of the wing, and was built up when the newel stair, which crossed it, was altered.

Brief History

The estate belonged anciently to the family of Balfour and was originally called Balorr, which was derived from its situation near the Ore. It passed to the Bethunes, by marriage in 1360.

In 1507 the lands of Balfour with others were confirmed to John Betoun of Balfoure and erected into a barony.

It was the seat of Admiral C. R. D. Bethune, and contained an original portrait of Cardinal Beaton. The Cardinal's ghost supposedly haunted the castle, and there is a compelling story surrounding the death of the Reverend John Pinkerton. He was an overnight guest on 16th June 1784. The next morning he was found at the foot of the stairs with a look of absolute terror on his face. It is presumed to have seen the Cardinal's ghost, and being a protestant minister did the Cardinal have his revenge ?

Balfour was, reputedly, the trysting place

Balfour — before destruction

of Mary, Queen of Scots, and Henry, Lord Darnley. It appears that the Queen rode down from Falkland Palace to meet Darnley from Wemyss Castle at Balfour for their romancing. The Queen is said to have planted four trees on a knoll near the castle where they used to meet (The Queen's Knowe). Neither the knoll nor the trees are still in existence, but the line of the original road from Wemyss to Balfour is still a right of way.

The castle was blown up in the 1960s

Balfour – today

7 Maiden Castle

Ordnance Survey (OSR) = NO 349015

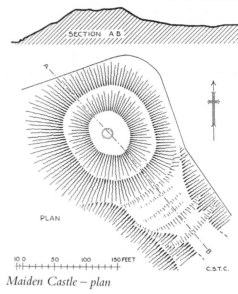

Return to the main road in Milton of Balgonie, and turn right. Turn right again on the A911 (to Leven). After 1 Km (2/3 mile), take the left turn to Windygates, and then left again at the traffic lights on the A916. Kennoway is 1 Km (2/3 mile) away. Park on the right in a clearing just after the Burns Tavern and take a short walk.

Maiden Castle – plan

Structure

The summit of the knoll is planted around the margin with trees, and the slopes on the west, south-west and south are covered with a growth of whins. Around the slopes there are indications of a slight terracing, and a flattening of the ridge suggests that there has been an approach from the south or south-east. The summit of the knoll is roughly circular. In the centre is a circular depression, about one metre in depth and six metres in diameter.

Brief History

The site is traditionally associated with "Macduff, Thane of Fife", but in the early 12th century Kennoway had been granted Merleswain and therefore more likely that he or a descendant had raised the motte.

Maiden Castle

8 MacDuff's Castle

Ordnance Survey (OSR) = NT 344972

Return on the A916, and turn left at the traffic lights. At the roundabout turn right on the A915 towards Kirkcaldy, and stay on this road for 1.5 Km (1 mile). Turn left on the B930 to Buckhaven, and then right on the A955. After a further 1.5 Km (1 mile) park in the Macduff cemetery and walk on the footpath signed Buckhaven to the ruin.

Structure

Also known as Kennoway castle and Thanes Castle, it is situated just east of the village of East Wemyss. A century ago there were the remains of two rectangular towers, but now only the red sand-stoned western tower of the castle is clearly visible. It contained five storeys with large square windows.

Besides the wall on the east enclosing the courtyard, the castle was surrounded on three sides by a wall of defence pierced with loopholes. The landward wall had a tower at each corner, but only the one at the west end remains. There appears to have been a postern in the western wall leading down to the sea. There are the remains of what seem older buildings close to the cliffs overhanging the sea, which also housed two of the famous Wemyss caves containing cup markings.

Brief History

Sir John of Methil and Wemyss, who assumed the family name of Wemyss, possibly built the first stone castle on this site. That castle was burnt to the ground on the orders of Edward I. Sometime after the Battle of Bannockburn, it was rebuilt into a single keep.

On the death of Sir Michael Wemyss about 1342, the estates were divided between his three daughters, one of whom married a Livingstone. Their right to live in the castle was challenged by Dame Margaret of Glen, but through an agreement the Livingstones continued to inhabit. In 1530 they exchanged estates with Sir James Colville, and the Colvilles lived at East Wemyss for 100 years.

On the death of the 2nd Lord Colville in 1630, the lands were purchased by Sir John, 1st Earl of Wemyss who reunited the Wemyss Estate. It was occupied until 1666, when Lady Jean Wemyss, Countess of Sutherland, asked to allow her children to play there.

Falling ruinous thereafter, it was not until 1906 that the Laird, Randolph Wemyss, took steps for the conservation of the castle, and during that work the arms of the Colville family were found in the sand.

MacDuff's Castle

9 Wemyss Castle

Ordnance Survey (OSR) = NT 329951

> Continue on the A955 through East We-
> myss and Coaltown of Wemyss, and turn
> left after 3Km (2 miles) signposted West
> Wemyss and then car park / harbour.
> Keep left at the Belvedere Hotel to the
> eastern end and the car park. Walk along
> the beach to view Wemyss Castle from
> the rear.

Structure

The castle is also known as "Hall of the Wemyss". Its oldest part, which is the oblong
tower forming a re-entrant in the west front,
has been so altered that its date cannot be ex-
actly determined. It may be considered not
later than the end of the 15th century.

The area between the tower and the cliffs
on north and east was probably enclosed by
curtain walls, in places supporting lean-to

Wemyss Castle

buildings, and the lowest part of the present
south wall as well as the drum-tower covering the north-west angle of the enclosure may
be the remains of these structures. If so, the
original castle occupied only the northern

part of the site now built upon, and, until the
17th century, there were no buildings south
of the tower.

In the 16th century the walls of enclosure
were rebuilt with a salient round tower on
the south-east, a rounded projection at the
eastern angle, and a vaulted entrance set between the main tower and that on the south-
east.

The construction of the entrance shows that
there was at least one chamber above it.
Against the curtain-walls on north, east, and
west lay other buildings, which with the tower
enclosed a small courtyard.

Most of the castle is constructed of rubble
and was covered with harling, but the main
tower is of ashlar in courses fairly cubical.

The ground floor of the buildings on the
east and that of the main tower are vaulted.
The 16th century kitchen most likely lay
against the north wall of the enclosure.

At the northern end of the 17th century
extension is a stately scale-and-platt staircase
of oak, dating
from the same
century.

Brief History

The origin of the
Wemyss family
was derived from
the family of
Macduff, Thane
of Fife in the reign
of Malcolm
Ceannmor.

During the
Wars of Independ-
ence the Wemyss
family initially
supported Edward I.
There is preserved in Wemyss a large silver
basin, which was given in 1290 by the King
of Norway to Sir Michael Wemyss of Wemyss, on occasion of that knight and Sir
Michael Scott of Balwearie appearing at the

Norwegian court as ambassadors from Scotland to bring home the Princess Margaret, for her proposed marriage to Edward II.

As the war progressed they changed their allegiance to Robert the Bruce, which caused Edward I to seek revenge by sacking the castle.

The castle was enlarged by Sir John Wemyss to house his royal visitors, and he was a great supporter of Mary, Queen of Scots who met Darnley for the first time within its walls in 1565.

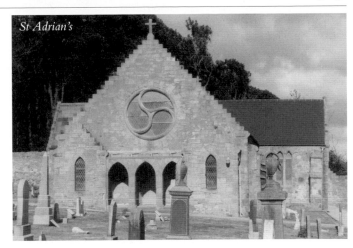

St Adrian's

Sir John's grandson was elevated to the title of Earl of Wemyss, Elcho and Methil in 1633 and, before his death in 1649, he had been both High Commissioner to the General Assembly and a Privy Councillor. It was, however, his son David, the second Earl, who was finally to establish the reputation and fortunes of the family.

He did not become directly involved in Scotland's politics, but did play host to Charles II, who spent a day in Wemyss Castle in July 1650, shortly after he had been proclaimed King, and again just before the disastrous Battle of Worcester, which resulted in the occupation of Scotland by Cromwell. The King also slept a night there in July 1657.

After the Restoration in 1660 and the return of more settled times, he embarked on a comprehensive building programme to create more space for his three successive wives and seventeen children. Despite only two daughters surviving childhood, the youngest did marry her cousin Sir James Wemyss, and kept the title in the family.

The third and fourth Earls further enhanced the family fortunes by marrying the eldest daughter of the Duke of Queensberry and of Drumlanrig and the daughter of the wealthy Charteris of Amisfield respectively.

David, the fourth Earl, was an ardent Jacobite and following the defeat of the Jacobites at Culloden, he was forced to flee to Switzerland, where he died in 1787. This led to the break-up of the Wemyss title and estates with his next brother, Francis, assuming the title and the Charteris estates, and his younger brother, James, the estates and Castle of Wemyss.

James's grandson married Millicent, the forceful grand-daughter of William IV, and on her husband's death in 1864 she took over the running of the estate with considerable success for the next 30 years.

> Before leaving you make sure to visit St Adrian's church next to the car park

10 West Wemyss Castle

Ordnance Survey (OSR) = NT 319947

From the car park return through the village keeping left to aim for the parking area at the very western end which looks like a small harbour. It is very peaceful, and there is an abundance of terns diving for food at the right time of year. The castle is a short walk along the path next to the shore.

Structure

Facing the sea are the remains of a good 16th century house, which has been four storeys and a garret in height. On plan it is oblong with a stair tower projecting from the middle of the south front, the tower being rounded in the lower part and corbelled out to the square at the top storey, where there was a little chamber. On the east side of the tower there is a single shot-hole. The masonry throughout is of coursed rubble, probably once harled.

The entrance to the house lies in the stair-tower. On the ground floor are two vaulted chambers – the eastern one was the kitchen and the western one was a cellar. Within the vault there has been an entresol floor. On the first floor the staircase opened into a traverse passage, latterly communicating with the garden behind. On the west of the passage lay the hall, which retains a vestige of the fireplace in its south wall and, beside the fireplace, an aumbry with ogival head. Breaches in the south and west wall presumably represent accesses to the hanging gallery.

The wall in front of the house, separating the property from the shore, dates in part from the 16th century. The tower at the western end and the outlook or bastion between the towers are also of the 16th century.

Brief History

In 1536 Sir Patrick Jackson spent £1000 on the chapel and manse and the Laird of Wemyss granted it certain lands. After the Reformation the Chapel was deserted as a place of worship, but in 1627, when David Lord Elcho (later 2nd Earl of Wemyss) was married to the Honourable Anna Balfour, the Chapel was converted into a place of residence. Lord Elcho laid out the gardens which today contain the Wemyss family burial ground. The late Randolph Erskine Wemyss lies here as does the body of Lord Wester Wemyss, who was Admiral of the Fleet and 1st Lord of the Admiralty at the close of World War 1.

West Wemyss

11 Ravenscraig Castle

Ordnance Survey (OSR) = NT 291925

Exit the village and return to the A955. Turn left towards Kirkcaldy, and join the B929. (There is a left turn after 3 Km (1.9 miles) to Dysart which is a very interesting village. Details can be found on page 75). In another 1 Km (0.7 miles) there is Ravenscraig Park where you can park, and there is a short walk to the castle.

Ravenscraig Castle stands on a rocky promontory running out into the Firth of Forth. On three sides it is protected by the sea, from which the rock rises sheer up about 90 metres.

Structure

The building belongs to the 15th century, and is all of one age. It consists of a keep at the north-west angle, presenting a rounded front towards the mainland. A curtain extends eastwards from the keep, where it joins a projecting round tower, forming the north-east angle of the castle. The entrance is in the centre of the curtain, through a broadly splayed round arched doorway. The vaulted entrance passage leads to the courtyard, and on either side of the passage are vaulted cellars.

These cellars project into the courtyard beyond the inner face of the keep, and this space opposite the keep is occupied by a fore court and staircase leading to the first floor. At the top of the fore stair, and in the south-east corner of the keep, a newel stair leads to the two upper floors and an attic.

The north-east round tower, like the keep, is square towards the courtyard. A vaulted passage rising a few steps leads to the room on the ground floor. This seems to have been the hall for ordinary use. The above passage also gives access to the turnpike leading to the upper floors and battlements of this wing.

There appears to have been an open paved platform over the entrance passage, and the cellars on each side of it, while the curtain is carried up as a screen wall, and is pierced with two horizontal embrasures for guns. There is also in each recess a slot-hole on each side.

Ravenscraig Castle

These were in all probability intended to receive the ends of the bars to which the guns were attached to prevent their recoil.

The enclosing walls round the top of the rock remain only in portions here and there. They have been ornamented with corbels similar to those of the curtain.

At the extreme end of the rock are the remains of a rounded bastion, and at the north-

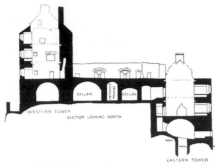

Ravenscraig Castle – section

west corner there seems to been a postern entering from the ditch. The passage from the postern is between the keep and enclosing wall, and has long been built over. A wall on the very edge of the precipice above the beach is loopholed.

Brief History

Ravenscraig or Ravensheugh Castle was built originally for Mary of Gueldres, the Queen of James II, and was designed by the Royal Master Mason, Henry Merlzioun. The lands including the site were acquired by the Queen in march 1460, their original possessors receiving an equivalent in lands belonging to her elsewhere. In 1461 the structure was sufficiently advanced to accommodate the Queen's Steward and other servants. Queen Mary died on 1st December 1463, and seven years later King James III granted the castle with the neighbouring lands to William, Earl of Caithness and Lord St. Clair, in partial recompense for the castle of Kirkwall and the earldom of Orkney. It continued to be inhabited by the St. Clairs (Sinclairs) on a regular basis until the 17th century by when it probably declined in favour, although the building remained in their possession until 1896.

Castle is open all year.
Tel: 0131 668 8800

Ravenscraig Castle

12 Seafield Tower

Ordnance Survey (OSR) = NT 280885

Exit the car park and turn left, and keep left on the A921 skirting Kirkcaldy by the coast. (Turn right at the Mercat Centre for convenient parking for the town centre. Details of Kirkcaldy town centre can be found on page 76). At the southern end turn left at the roundabout, and then first left into Seafield Road. Keep right to the parking area by the coast. The Castle can be seen from the car park, and is accessible along the coastal path.

Structure

It was built on a rock on the foreshore, beside a burn, and the rock has been cut in places to a vertical face, as much to provide building material as for protection.

What remains of the tower stands free from the boundary walls and is L-shaped on plan, comprising a main block and a wing, the latter being an addition to contain the staircase. Apparently the addition replaced a smaller stair-wing. Its building blocked up the original entrance to the ground floor, and a new entrance had to be formed in the eastern wall. The masonry is rubble and regularly coursed and heavily grouted.

The ground floor is vaulted and has had an entresol floor of wood inserted at the springing-level. The lower part has been subdivided. At its south-west corner the remains of a hatch through the vault can be traced, and a small fireplace at the same corner seems to have been inserted; the two narrow windows looking northward, which lit the upper and lower part of the ground floor, are original. The first floor was a single chamber with a large fireplace in the north gable and windows to east and south, the latter provided with window-seats in the deep embrasures. At the southern corners of the room are ruinous mural chambers, the western probably a garderobe, the eastern a lobby served by the original stair. Above are two upper floors, in which the arrangement has been roughly similar.

Brief History

It was probably built by John Moutray of Seafield around the mid 16th century. The lands of Seafield were associated with the Constableship of Kinghorn in early times.

Seafield Tower

John de Kirkcauldy held Seafield in 1440. It was a property of the Moultray family, and probably continued in use until the last laird was killed in the Jacobite Rising of 1715, after which the lands passed to the Earl of Melville.

13 Grange

Ordnance Survey (OSR) = NT 270886

Return to the main road, and turn left on the A921, and the first right is a track to Grange. It is a working farm and therefore you should view from a distance.

Grange

Structure

The farmhouse contains all that remains of the mansion of the 16th century. It is a round tower with stringcourses and gunloop, but the door at the foot of the tower is modern. A doorway, now enclosed by modern work on the north side of the main block, bears an inscribed lintel dated 1687 and the monogram I S M.

Brief History

Grange is memorable as the seat of Sir James Kirkcaldy of Grange, Lord High Treasurer to James V and to Queen Mary. He was probably descended from George de Kirkcaldy,

Grange

who held the lands of Tyrie and Seafield previous to 1440. Sir James Kirkcaldy obtained the castle of Kinghorn in 1540 from James V after the forfeiture of Lord Glamis; and in the same year the King confirmed to him the lands, tower, and fortalice of Grange, erecting it into a free barony, "for services done by him in France, and elsewhere outwith the kingdom". After the forfeiture of Sir James the estate was conferred on David Hamilton, third son of the Governor Arran, in 1547; but in 1564, when Parliament reduced the sentence of forfeiture, Grange was bestowed upon Sir James' son, William Kirkcaldy. The heroic efforts of the latter to defend the interests of Queen Mary are recorded in every history of his time. He was ultimately executed by the orders of the Regent Morton, who seized upon the forfeited estate of Grange and bestowed it upon his own illegitimate son, William Douglas. The Regent suffered retributive justice for his crimes, and the estate then was conferred on Esme Stewart, Duke of Lennox.

14 *Inchkeith*

Ordnance Survey (OSR) = NT 293828

(At the time of going to press, there seems to be no means of reaching the island of Inchkeith, however if it was possible the Kinghorn should be the start point). Return to the main road, and turn right on the A921, and head for the pier in Kinghorn.

Alternatively, just as you are entering Kinghorn, branch right on the B923, and take the first right after 1 Km (0.5 miles). Travel for 2 Km (1.25 miles) on this minor road, until you reach some crossroads. Turn right, and within a few hundred metres you can see Pitteadie Castle (No 15, page 28) on your left.

Structure

All that remains is a stretch of rubble masonry wall, with gunloops, which was part of the outer wall on the north-east side. Beneath the signal tower is a core of rubble, which may be a 16th century structure.

An armorial panel bearing the Royal arms has been inserted over the entrance to the

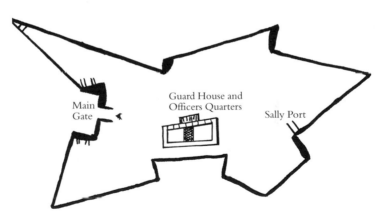

Inchkeith – 16th century French fort

courtyard of the lighthouse. The shield seems to be enclosed within an Order, and beneath it are painted the initials of M(aria) R(egina), while lower down is the date 1564, carved in relief and also painted.

Brief History

A fort was constructed upon Inchkeith by the English during their occupation of the island, following the battle of Pinkie, in the early part of 1549, but, as it was raised within a fortnight, it can have been only a temporary structure of timber and earth. After the recovery of the island, however, it was again fortified in 1550 on behalf of the Scots, by their allies the French, under the command of the Sieur D'Esse. The French mercenaries were left to guard Inchkeith in the interests of Queen Mary, and remained there until 1560.

The Parliament of 1567 ordered the demolition of the place, but because the order was not strictly complied with much of it still existed in 1773, when Dr Johnson visited the island and found a fort there. In 1803, however, most of this was removed, when a lighthouse was erected on the site.

The notion of fortifying Inchkeith was frequently brought under the notice of the Government about the time of the Crimean War. The island was purchased from the Duke of Buccleuch, and by 1878 three polygonal batteries had been constructed on the three promontories, and they effectively commanded the entrance to the Firth of Forth and the south-eastern shore of Fife.

15 Pitteadie Castle

Ordnance Survey (OSR) = NT 257891

Return along the A921 eastwards until the road meets the B923. Turn left and then take the first right after 1 Km (0.5 miles). Travel for 2 Km (1.25 miles) on this minor road, until you reach some crossroads. Turn right, and within a few hundred metres you can see Pitteadie Castle on your left.

Structure

The castle is a free-standing oblong tower, originally built probably towards the end of the 15th century but considerably altered two centuries later.

The tower is built of rubble, with dressings at the voids. There are three storeys beneath the wall-head, and there is evidence of an attic and garret within the roof.

The south-east angle is carried up as a two-storeyed cap-house, and there is a turret-stair within the re-entrant. At the north-eastern and south-western angles were "rounds", only the corbelling for which survives. The original entrance, which was at first-floor level, may still be traced on the south wall in the remains of an arched doorway with corbels for a wooden landing.

In the more important alterations of the 17th century an entrance was formed at the

ground level, the former entrance being built up.

The ground floor is vaulted. The first floor has a window looking north. The second floor was divided into two rooms in the 17th century. In its east gable there are traces of the 15th century fireplace.

Brief History

In 1519 John Vallance ("Wallangis") was served heir to his father David in Easter and Wester Pitteadie, as separate holdings in the barony of Easter Kinghorn. The original tower was apparently built by his family. Subsequently the lands were in possession of a family named Sandilands, but in 1612 they

Pitteadie Castle

were erected into a barony in favour of John Boswell. To the Boswells may be attributed the 17th century reconstructions. In 1710 Pitteadie belonged to a "gentleman of the name of Calderwood".

16 Balwearie Castle

Ordnance Survey (OSR) = NT 251903

Balwearie Castle

Continue on the minor road, and take the first left, and then right towards Kirkcaldy and pick up the A907. In 1 Km (0.5 miles), pass under the railway bridge, and at the next roundabout take the left turn (B925) to Auchtertool. In 2 Km (1.25 miles) take a left turn at Boglily on a minor road. Follow this road for 1 Km (0.5 miles) and then turn right at the junction and Balwearie Castle is just through the farmyard on your left.

Structure

Balwearie Castle has been an oblong 15th century tower. The north gable and east wall, as well as part of the south wall, still stand fairly complete to their wall-heads. The masonry is ashlar built in courses with very tenacious shell-lime, and is fairly cubical towards the base of the walls. The voids are chamfered externally. A parapet-walk, borne on separate corbels of two members, has returned round the walls.

The accommodation comprised a ground floor, with an entresol beneath its vault, and three upper storeys.

The ground floor vault is of ashlar. The windows on the ground and entresol floors are narrow, and only the entresol windows are furnished with stone seats. There is a garderobe with lamp recess and vent in the north wall of the entresol floor. The hall on the first floor has a garderobe in the north wall and windows with seats to north, east and south.

The second floor seems to have been divided into two rooms of unequal size. The southern room, which is the larger, contains traces of an unusually ample fire-place with jambs and furnished with moulded capitals and bases.

On the third floor the fire-place lintel has been supported on corbels, while the windows have been small in size and set between the corbels of the parapet.

Brief History

Sir Michael Scott is noted in 1280 as heir of Sir Richard of Balwearie. On 23 February 1463/4 James III granted to William Scott of Balwearie free faculty and special licence to erect a castle or fortalice on his lands of Balwearie.

Sir Michael was acclaimed as a wizard who could fly, make himself invisible, predict death and even conjure up the Devil. Little is known about his early life, but he was born in the Borders in 1175. His intellect led him to Oxford, Paris and Bologna. In 1220 he was summoned to the court of Emperor Frederick at Palermo.

17 Hallyards Castle

Ordnance Survey (OSR) = NT 212914

Return to the main road. Turn left on the B925 to Auchtertool and turn right in the village to Lochgelly. On this minor road, the scant ruins of Hallyards Castle can be seen after 1 Km (0.5 miles) on your left in a ploughed field.

Structure

Some fragments of walling and a few mounds rising with a ploughed field represent all that remains of Hallyards Castle, which has evidently been an extensive house of the 16th or 17th century, built round a courtyard. A somewhat less ruinous structure at the north-east corner is possibly of later date. Part of the gable at the south-east corner, indicated that here the building had been a vaulted ground-floor and at least two upper floors.

Hallyards Castle

Brief History

A seat of the Kirkcaldys of Grange, it gave a night's lodging to James V, on his way to Falkland after the defeat of Solway Moss (1542). In 1539 George Brown, bishop of Dunkeld, granted to Sir James "– and the lands and lake of Halyairdis". His successor, Sir William Kirkcaldy of Grange, resided at Hallyards, as in 1565 he signed a charter there. Early in the 17th century the barony of Auchtertool was acquired by Sir Andrew Skene of Auchrie and in 1653 John Skene of Hallyards was retoured as heir of his father, Sir Andrew. To confirm that taken from the diary of Mr John Lamont of Newton – "1653, January – The old laird of Halyeards in Fyfe (surnamed Skine), depairted out of this life att Halyeards, and was interred att Achtertoole church." The widow survived until 1670. The property remained in possession of the Skenes until the end of the 18th century. David Skene's elder son Robert represented Fifeshire in Parliament from 1780 to 1787. Succession fell to the elder daughter, Helen, mother to Patrick Moncrieff of Reidie and Myres Castle. It is said to have been the rendezvous of the leading Fife Jacobites at the rebellion of 1715.

18 Carden Tower

Ordnance Survey (OSR) = NT 226937

Continue northwards on the minor road for 2 Km (1.25 miles), until you meet the junction with Loch Gelly on your left. Turn right and pass Shawsmill, and after emerging from a long S bend, there is sufficient space on the left hand side to park at the entrance to a Forestry Authority plantation. Walk for 300 metres (0.25 miles) through the wood, and as you enter a clearing and the path follows the stream to the left, you will see a series of wooden steps to your right. Climb the steps to the top but before you walk along the ridge to Carden Tower, go straight on to the gate posts, a few yards/ metres away. Here you will see a marker dated 23rd August 1826 denoting "The Last Duel in Scotland"

Structure

All that remains of this tower is a right-angled fragment of walling standing on the precipitous right bank of the Gelly Burn overlooking Cardenden. It was an appropriate ancient name, Carden meaning "high fortified place". The building has been a small 16th house, and recent excavations have shown that it was of an L-shaped plan and containing at least three storeys, the lowest of which may have been vaulted.

The only feature of any interest remaining is a ruinous "round" at the south-west angle which is borne on a continuous corbelling of four members; the round has been provided with shot-holes pointing downwards.

The masonry is rubble, but the round and its corbel are of ashlar.

Brief History

In 1482 John "Mertyne" or Martin of Midhope, West Lothian, granted the land of "Cardwan", in the constabulary of Kinghorn, to his son Henry. The direct line of the Martins of Midhope came to an end, and in 1582 the King conferred on George "Martene" the lands of "Cardoun" with tower, manor place, etc which had been in the royal hands for about 50 years. The tower had been erected subsequently to 1482 and before 1532. These Martins also failed, and in 1623 David Wemyss was served heir to his father in the lands and barony of "Cardowan".

It passed through different owners during the 17th century, and became derelict by the 1720s. The remains were almost lost to recent open-cast mining which saw the ruin nearly buried by spoil heaps.

The Corrie Centre Local History Group restored the site as part of the Council for Scottish Archaeology's Adopt-a-Monument Scheme with assistance from Fife Regional Council and Kirkcaldy District Council.

Carden Tower

19 *Lochore Castle*

Ordnance Survey (OSR) = NT 175959

Lochore Castle

south-eastern angles there have been small rounded towers, which seem to have been added in the 16th century, and are today almost entirely demolished.

The entrance to the barmkin-enclosure was on the north-west through an arched doorway.

The ground floor is filled with debris and is inaccessible. On the first floor is the entrance, which opened from the west into a small lobby within the thickness of the wall. Beyond lay the hall which had a mural chamber beside the door.

Returning to the car, return westwards on the minor to the roundabout on the north side of Loch Gelly. Pass over the A92, and straight across the next roundabout, but turn left at the next roundabout, and into Lochgelly. At the next junction turn right on the B920. In 2.1 Km (1.5 miles) there is a left turn into Lochore Meadows Country Park where the castle is situated. Details of the Country Park, with a map, can be found on page 78.

Structure

Eighteenth century records describe the site as a peninsula, but it may well be that it was originally an island, a view supported by the old Gaelic name of the property, which was "Inch-gall".

Present appearances suggest that the original castle had been of the motte-and-bailey type. The base of the mound has been enclosed by a barmkin of coursed rubble, now fragmentary.

At the north-eastern, north-western and

Brief History

Grose, Cardonnel and others suppose it to have been built in the 12th century by Duncan de Lochore. It remained in the family through the 13th century (in 1255 David de Lochore was one of the Scottish magnates). Later on, in the reign of Robert I, the lands came to the son of a gentleman, Adam de Valloniis, who had married a daughter of the Barons of Lochor. It remained in this family, until the eldest daughter of D. Jacobus de Valloniis married Sir Andrew Wardlaw of Torry, and with her he got Wester-Lochoreshire, or the parish of Ballingry, whose church is an old parsonage at the laird of Lochor's presentation. Wardlaw of Torry kept the barony of Lochor till King Charles I's time, and their chief mansion was the castle of Lochor, consisting of a strong tower and many lower houses, all enclosed with a wall, that is washed with the water of the loch. In 1662 there is a *novodamus* charter of the lands of "Inchgall" or lochore to John "Malcomb" of Balbedie.

20 Strathendry Castle

Ordnance Survey (OSR) = NO 226020

> Return to the main road, and turn left on the B920. In 2.5 Km (1.5 miles), join the B9097, but keep travelling north on the B920 when the two roads separate, for 4 Km (2.5 miles). Turn right on the A911 at Scotlandwell. In 4 Km (2.5 miles) there is a left turn to Strathendry. Following a very rough track the castle can be viewed from the rear and outside the gates.

The current owners are Iain and Margaret Maciver. Ever since Iain was a small boy, he had a dream of living in a castle. Unexpectedly, in 1987, he saw Strathendry for sale in a magazine. Although the castle was at the other side of Scotland, he persuaded a somewhat reluctant spouse to travel through that afternoon to view it. They bought it, even though for the next six years Iain drove 140 miles a day to work and back - he was that keen to buy a castle! They began a long term programme of renovation, particularly of the near derelict steading buildings, cottages and overgrown walled garden, and they did much of the work themselves. The 16th century keep was in much better condition, although many of the principal rooms have been refurbished and redecorated. The renovation of the small kirk in the grounds commenced in 1996, to be followed by converting part of the steading building into a Clan centre. The Clan Iver Society is already based at the castle. The initiation of the Clan Centre in conjunction with Clan Forrester, whose ancestors built the castle, is the next objective.

Structure

It is oblong on plan and contains three storeys and an attic. The stair-tower probably replaces an original but smaller stair in the same position. The eastern gable is surmounted by a bartizan, with open rounds at the angles, set forward on a corbel table of later 16th century type. The gables are crowstepped.

The northern entrance, set in the western side of the stair tower, displays a monogram of the initials S. E. D., probably for Sir E. Douglas, a younger son of Douglas of Kirkness, who married the Forrester heiress and so acquired the property. The monogram is flanked by the date 1699.

Brief History

Forrester, a son of Carden's, married the heiress, and it continued in the name of Forrester until Charles II. Thomas Forrester of "Strathanrye" is on record in 1516 as sheriff-depute of Fife.

Strathendry Castle

21 Corston Tower

Ordnance Survey (OSR) = NO 208098

Return to the main road and turn right on the A911. Stay on the A road for 8 Km (5 miles), until you meet the B919. Drive for 3 Km (2 miles) to the junction with the A91. Turn right and proceed for 6 Km (4 miles) and the ruins of Corston are on your right. There is a lay-by on the right-hand side of the road.

Corston Tower – before the walls fell

Structure

The shell of this 16th century tower contains the east wall still standing to the height of the third floor windows. The remains of the other walls are inconsiderable. The masonry is of rubble with ashlar dressings.

The tower was three full storeys, with a storey in the roof, and a watch-tower placed over the staircase, which occupied the south-west corner. The ground floor only was vaulted. The joists of the upper floors were of black oak, and the roof was covered with heavy pavement slabs. On the second floor a garderobe still exists at the north-east corner, with an exit at the ground level.

There were outbuildings connected with the tower on the west side, of which traces of foundations remain. The kitchen was a detached one-storey building and it stood at the south-west corner.

Brief History

In the 15th century Corston belonged to John Ramsay, who was descended from the house of Carnock. His son, Sir John of Corston, received from James III the barony and lordship of Bothwell, with the title of Lord Bothwell, the lands and dignity being confirmed by Parliament in 1483. The lands of Corston remained in the possession of the Ramsays until about 1669, when they passed into the hands of a family named Colquhoun. At the end of the 19th century to the Marquis of Bute, shortly after the whole structure,

Corston Tower

22 Pitcairlie

Ordnance Survey (OSR) = NO 236148

Continue on the A91 for 3 Km (2 miles) into Auchtermuchty. Take the left turn on the B936 in the town centre to Cupar. Pitcairlie is 3 Km (2 miles) on the left. It is easily viewed from the road side.

Structure

The mansion which stands on an eminence, is a composite structure, greatly altered in the 18th century and again about 1800, but still retaining a late 16th century basis, the extent and arrangement of which cannot now be accurately determined. The western part and a rectangular tower projecting from the southern angle are definitely of the earliest period.

The house is three storeys in height, rubble-built and harled. The tower is surmounted by an ashlar parapet with rounds, and has a turret-stair corbelled out at second floor level within the western re-entrant angle. The present entrance faces northeast and opens into a modernised hall, which originally formed three apartments (now two); beyond is a vaulted passage, from which are entered two vaulted chambers, the smaller opening into the lower part of the tower. The stair, which rises at the western end of the hall, is modern, and there is no trace of the original access to the upper floors.

On the first floor, the drawing room occupies the front of the house and contains impressive French paintings representing the four seasons (photograph on the rear cover), and on the western side of the passage are three chambers, the two northern of which were originally one room. The southern chamber communicated with a chamber in the tower, which was panelled in Memel pine of the 18th century, and there are traces of a similar finish in the other rooms. On the second storey the tower-room and the smoking-room, which was above the drawing room, are panelled; the other rooms have been modernised, but one contains a simply moulded stone fireplace, which is original.

Brief History

Like Mugdrum and Easter Lumbenny, the lands of Pitcairlie formerly belonged to the parish of Abernethy, and was part of the barony of Ballinbreich. "The lands of Petcarlings" belonged to the Abernethy family in early times, and were given c1296 by Sir Alexander de Abernethy to Sir John de Moravia of Tullibardine. Sir Alexander was one of the Scottish nobles who joined Bruce in his opposition to Edward I, but he latterly espoused the cause of the English monarch and was appointed governor of the castle of Dundee, which he garrisoned and held for Edward and his successor. His lands were forfeited and bestowed by Robert I on "his be

Pitcairlie

loved son Robert". The sentence of forfeiture does not seem to have been carried out, however, as the three daughters of Sir Alexander Abernethy had the lands that belonged to their father divided among them. Sir Andrew Leslie, ancestor of the Earls of Rothes, was married about 1312 to Mary, daughter of Sir Alexander, and with her obtained the lands of Pitcairlie, which were joined to the barony of Ballinbreich. Andrew, 4th Earl of Rothes , gave Pitcairlie to his son Sir Patrick Leslie, who afterwards became 1st Lord Lindores. His son David served in the army of Gustavus Adolphus, and gained his soldiership there. At the battle of Marston Moor, 1644, he fought along with Cromwell against Charles I, and by a dashing charge of cavalry which he commanded he was prominent in deciding the fate of the battle. In 1645 he discomfited Montrose at Philiphaugh, and in 1650 he was appointed Commander-in-Chief,

Pitcairlie

when the Earl of Leven resigned. He positioned his army between Cromwell and Edinburgh, and then occupied the heights above Dunbar, but subsequently was routed by Cromwell. David adhered to the falling fortunes of Charles II, and shared with him the battle of Worcester in 1651. He was detained prisoner by Cromwell for a year or two. After the restoration of Charles II, he created Lord Newark, and Newark Castle at St Monans is the only remaining memo of David Leslie's toils, title and estates. In 1649, money affairs were left in a state of confusion, and eventually Pitcairlie was adjudged by the Court of Session in 1667 to John Bayne, one of the creditors on the estate. Colonel James Cathcart of Carbiston acquired Pitcairlie about the middle of the 18th century, and his grand-nephew, James Taylor Cathcart, was retoured as heir in 1760. James Cathcart of Carbiston died unmarried, and James Taylor Cathcart died in 1795. Major James Cathcart, eldest son of the latter, after a distinguished military career in India, died unmarried in 1810, when the succession fell to his brother Robert Cathcart, captain in the Royal Navy. Robert served with great distinction under Admiral Nelson both at the Nile and in the Baltic. He was married in 1814 to Catherine, daughter of Henry Scrymgeour Wedderburn of Wedderburn and Birkhill, but died without issue in 1833. His brother, Taylor Cathcart, succeeded to the estate, and at his death in 1857 his eldest surviving son, Robert, became laird of Pitcairlie. He was appointed Vice- Lieutenant of Fifeshire in 1886.

The current owners, Bill and Muriel Mclay have created five luxury self-catering holiday homes within the 120 acre country estate of park, meadowland, woods, streams and small ornamental lake. Guests are welcome to wander and relax in extensive grounds, children can enjoy making friends with the animals.

Pitcairlie

The Lodge (Sleeps 4)

This attractive south-facing Georgian cottage has been renovated to a high standard, comprising large sitting room with open fire, and separate dining area, well-fitted kitchen with door to garden and patio. Twin bedded room with wash basin, double bedroom with shower cubicle and wash basin. Bathroom and W.C.

The Eland Apartment (Sleeps 6)

This property consists of a spacious and elegant open plan sitting/dining room with well-equipped, modern fitted kitchen area. Double bedroom with en-suite shower room/W.C. Two twin bedrooms with en-suite shower room/W.C.

The Kudu Apartment (Sleeps 4)

Two-storey accommodation with six steps up to verandah and entrance. Cosy sitting/dining room with gas fire and small, well-equipped modern fitted kitchen area. Spiral stairs to the first floor with double bedroom with en-suite shower/W.C. Twin-bedded room with shower room/W.C.

The Garden Apartment (Sleeps 2/3)

This comfortable property offers accommodation all at ground floor level. Entrance from gardens to sitting room with gas fire. Well-fitted and equipped kitchen with dining area. Double bedroom. Single bedroom, bathroom/W.C.

The Sable Apartment (Sleeps 4)

This apartment offers comfortable accommodation on a split level, and is reached via 6 steps up to its verandah. Spacious open plan sitting/dining room with high vaulted ceiling, with gas fire and well-equipped modern fitted kitchen area. Double bedroom with en-suite shower room/W.C. Twin bedroom with en-suite shower room/W.C.

All properties have access to the indoor heated swimming pool.

For further details and colour brochure contact Heather Mclay, Pitcairlie House, Auchtermuchty, Fife KY14 6EU.
Tel: 01337 827418. Fax: 01337 828464.
Email: hmclay@pitcairlie.prestel.co.uk.

23 Myres Castle

Ordnance Survey (OSR) = NO 242110

Return southwards on the B936 to Auchtermuchty. Pass over the crossroads, keeping on the B936, where you will see Myres Castle on your right after roughly 1 Km (0.5 miles).

Structure

Mainly modern, it has grown from the small 16th century house of three storeys and an attic, which now forms its south-east corner. This consists of an oblong main block, with a stair-tower projecting from the north-west angle, a second tower projecting from the angle diametrically opposite, and a small turret, probably intended to contain a service stair corbelled out at the north-east angle. Presumably the entrance lay near the foot of the main staircase, where it would be covered by the oval gunloop still visible in the west wall of the main block.

The masonry is of harled rubble. The crow-steps of the west gable indicate the original level and show that the wall-head has been raised. On the south side it bears a moulded eaves-course and fascia of the later 17th century. The south-east tower is corbelled out to the square at second-floor level to support an upper part which is constructed in ashlar and is an addition. It terminates in a parapeted look-out reached from a turret-stair on the western side, the stair emerging from a caphouse crowned with a stone spire.

Brief History

When James I was held prisoner in England he became so attached to his young English page, Robert Coxwell, that he gave him the major portion of the royal property of Auchtermuchty, including Myres. He died in 1453 and the his widow married John Scrymgeour

In 1484 John Scrymgeour, second son of the Constable of Dundee, had a charter to this office, with the lands of the Myres of Auchtermuchty; and in 1531 his son, John Scrymgeour, Master of the King's Works, had a charter to all the lands of Myres. He was employed in the erection and repair of the palaces of Falkland and Holyrood.

By 1611 these lands had been transferred to Stephen Paterson and his wife Elizabeth Mure.

In 1628 John Paterson was served heir to his father, Michael Paterson of the Myris, in the lands of the Myris, Over and Nether, and also in the office of key-bearer. This office is attached to the lands, and has been held by the representatives of the various families who at different times have possessed Myres.

Directions to Falkland Palace (No 1)
Keep on the B936 south for 4 Km (2.5 miles) to Falkland, where the Palace is in the town centre (see page 3)

Castle Touring Guides

The West of Fife

Map 2 – The West of Fife

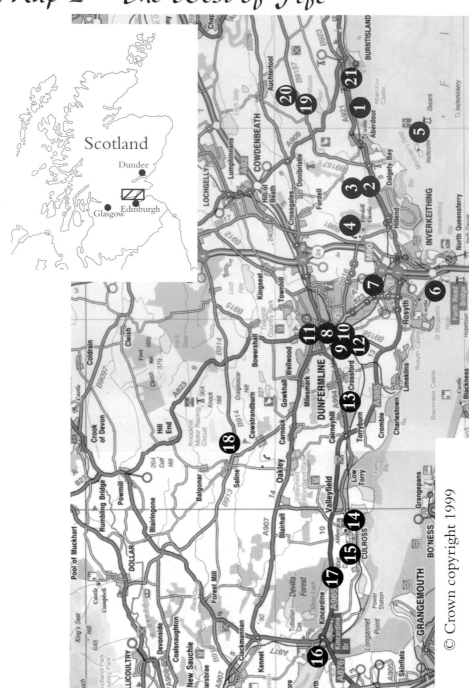

1 *Aberdour Castle*

Ordnance Survey (OSR) = NT 193854

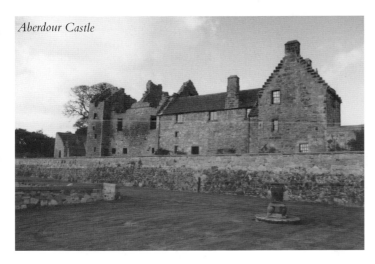
Aberdour Castle

Structure

The buildings may be dated to various periods from the 14th to the 17th century. The earliest stage is represented by the ruinous tower at the north-west, which has been a self-contained house of probably the 14th century, but which was altered in the second half of the 15th century and supplemented by an out-building. In the late 16th century the latter part was almost entirely destroyed and its remains were included in the western part of the present south range.

In the early 17th century a third range, which included a long gallery on the upper-floor, was run out eastwards from the south-east corner of the south range.

The eastern entrance to the garden bears in the pediment an earl's coronet and the date 1632 with a cartouche, on which are represented in monogram the initials of William, 7th Earl of Morton, and his Countess, Lady Anne Keith.

Little more than the ground floor of the old tower remains, but part of the south wall still stands to the wall-head. The masses of masonry, which lie in confusion on the west and south indicate the tenacity of the mortar.

At the first floor level there is another entrance in the south wall immediately above that on the ground floor, and to the west there was, until part of this wall collapsed, an original lancet-doublet, both lights being grouped beneath a semi-circular hood-mould.

The wall-head of the south wall terminated in a parapet-walk, having an external projection borne on a heavy triple-membered corbels and also an internal projection borne on corbels of a single member. Since the 15th century the roof of the tower has been flat or at most slightly pitched.

The structure south of the tower, which was added in the 15th century, has been almost entirely obliterated, but the foundation courses of the west wall of the 16th century newel stair, and its continuation farther south, are probably part of this structure, while the north wall of the 16th century south range contains traces of work older than that date.

The most westerly building of the castle is so fragmentary that its arrangement can only be conjectured. On the lowest floor there have been three chambers and a rounded projection on the north.

The 17th century addition built by the 7th Earl of Morton abuts on the east gable of the 16th century south range and communicates with it on the upper floor.

Brief History

It is possible that the square keep was erected by Thomas Randolph, Earl of Moray, the

Aberdour Castle – gallery

builder of Aberdour Castle. The tower of the Viponts may have survived till this period, but it may be taken as almost that the oldest part of the existing castle was built by "the Knight of Liddesdale". Sir William died without male issue in 1353, and was succeeded by his nephew, Sir James Douglas, ancestor of the Earls of Morton. When the latter title was created in 1457 it was conjoined with the minor title of Lord Aberdour. From a charter of 1452 it appears that it was then intended to have the castle repaired, though no trace of its reconstruction is found in contemporary documents. The first extension was made shortly before the execution of the Regent Morton in 1581. The Earls of Morton continued to hold this place until the middle of the 18th century.

brave companion of Robert the Bruce, and Regent of Scotland during the minority of David II. It is at least certain that this Earl was proprietor of the barony of Aberdour, and that he granted to the Abbey of Dunfermline the lands of Kulelauch (Cullaloe) that masses might be said for his uncle, King Robert the Bruce, and for his ancestors and successors. As this charter was confirmed by Robert I, it must have been granted previous to 1329. The Earl of Moray died in 1332. His two sons, Thomas and John, were successively Earls of Moray, and the first fell at the battle of Dupplin in 1332, while the second was slain at Durham in 1346. Their sister, the Countess of March ("Black Agnes") succeeded to the title as John, Earl of Moray, had died childless, but some time before his death the lands of Aberdour had passed mout of his possession. It is usually stated that John Randolph gave Aberdour to Sir William Douglas of Liddesdale in 1341, but it is certain that David II confirmed a charter to James Douglas at an earlier date. This would make the transferring of Aberdour during the lifetime of Thomas, the 1st Earl of Moray. It is noteworthy that the charter of 1341 merely confirms to Sir William Douglas of Liddesdale the gift which had been previously made. This narrows down the question as to the original

Open all year, except closed Thu PM and Fri Oct-Mar. Shop and cafe.
Tel: 01383 860519

2 Couston Castle

Ordnance Survey (OSR) = NT 193854

Head westwards out of Aberdour on the A921 for 1.5 Km (1 mile), and take a right turn which goes under the railway line. As you approach Otterston Loch Couston Castle is on your left behind the trees. No attempt should be made to enter the grounds.

Structure

Couston Castle was restored in 1985 to its 17th century form, when it was a L-plan tower house. It was three storeys with an attic, although the major portion of the main block was unusually two-storeyed. The masonry was of coursed rubble, the windows having their jambs and lintels rounded at the arris. The entrance, which was in the re-entrant angle and faced eastward, was a good 17th century door-piece, opening on the foot of a scale-and-platt stair, which rose to the first floor.

At the beginning of the 19th century, the castle was practically entire.

Brief History

At the beginning of the 17th century Couston belonged to the family of Logan, that being a branch of the old Midlothian family long located at Restalrig. In 1619 the King confirmed a charter of James Logan of Couston, son and heir of the late John Logan of Couston.

It formed the retreat of the Rev. Robert Blair, a well-known Presbyterian clergyman and outspoken opponent of Archbishop Sharp, whose life is detailed in Dr Ross's work "Aberdour and Inchcolm". The Reverend died there in 1666.

It is said that the original building was habitable around 1825, and view of the place though scarcely a vestige of the old structure remained circa 1895.

Couston

3 Otterston Tower

Ordnance Survey (OSR) = NT 165852

Otterston Tower – about 1895

> Continue on the minor road, and in 300 metres turn left on the private road. Otterston, or its remains, are some 200 metres down the track.

Structure

The present mansion is a large composite structure, the earliest part being the L-shaped central portion, or main block, which lies roughly east and west, with the wing projecting from its western end. This was the original house, built towards the close of the 16th century. The barmkin attached to the eastern wall of the wing and running northwards was probably an afterthought. Two of the towers which stood upon the barmkin still survive, and close to the more northerly of these is the entrance to the enclosure. In the 17th century two new wings were added within the barmkin, one as a westward con-

tinuation of the main block and the other as a prolongation of the original wing. Within modern times extensive additions were made on both sides of the old house, and these involved considerable internal alterations, among which was the gutting of the lower floors of the original wing to make room for a new staircase.

The entrance to the original house lay within the re-entrant angle. Just within the entrance was a good scale-staircase, which rose against the east wall of the main block to first floor level, from which the ascent was continued by a turret-stair corbelled out from the eastern gable; on the upper floors there was a passage above the scale-stair.

Above the entrance was a heavy stone corbelling which returned at the re-entrant angle along the eastern face of the wing. There were three floors within the main block and these were served by the two sets of stairs mentioned above.

Brief History

The original Otterston was built circa 1589. The lintel is dated such with the initials D. M. and L. M. which reflected the Moubray family. It was the property of Captain Moubray, R. N. in the early 19th century, whose ancestor, a cadet of the Barnbougle Moubray's, settled here in 1511 and owned 500 acres of the shire.

Otterston

4 *Fordell Castle*

Ordnance Survey (OSR) = NT 147854

Fordell Castle

which a passage leads to the other apartments. From one of these a stair leads up in the thickness of the wall to the dining-room or hall, as is almost universally the case, indicating that this was originally the wine-cellar.

On the first floor, the hall has a fireplace in the north wall, and is lighted by three windows. Beyond it is another chamber, occupying the remainder of this floor, and containing a garde-robe. An angle turret staircase is corbelled out at the south-east tower, and both of the towers contain rooms in their upper stages, the north-west one having an open battlement on the top, reached by a turret stair.

The arms are gules in a carved pointed frame, are those of the Hendersons, and below is a monogram of the letters IMH. In the centre of the base of the panel is the date 1567, with the letters H. E on one side, and I. H on the other. On the north-east skew stone is the date 1580, which is repeated over the doorway in the south-east tower. The picturesque corbelling of the towers, the dormer windows without parapet, and the small crow-stepped gables, are all well-marked features of the dates carved on the building.

Of all the minor details at Fordell, the most remarkable is a fine and unique gargoyle at the eaves. It is of lead, and represents a winged four-footed monster, with open mouth and defiant attitude, designed and executed with great spirit.

The castle was at one time enclosed with

Return to the A921, and turn right towards Inverkeithing. After 3 Km (2 miles), turn right on the B916. After 2 Km this road joins the B981, and within 500 metres take the right turn into the grounds. The castle is 1 Km on that road, but no attempt should be made to view without contacting the owners.

Structure

The building is designed on the Z-plan, but it has some peculiarities, in that the main building is a simple oblong with square towers at two of its opposite angles, each containing a wheel stair. There are two entrances, one in each tower, and these entrances and accompanying stairs are rather unusual in buildings of this class and date.

The ground floor, which is vaulted, contains three chambers, the east-most being the kitchen, the full width of the building, from walls, having a portcullis gate and drawbridge, but they were removed late in the 19th century.

These walls contained a considerable space of ground, and included a chapel dedicated to Saint Theriot, which, having become ruinous, was rebuilt on the same site in 1650. In the chapel there are German and Flemish influences with the 16th and 17th century stained glass roundels and fragments.

Brief History

About 1220 Richard, son of Hugh de Camera, presented to the Monastery of Inchcolm "thirteen acres of land in his territory of Fordell, lying near the sea, between the lands of Dalgety and the lands of Lowchald", together with a toft and croft in his town of Fordell. Fordell had been the seat of the Henrysons or Hendersons since the beginning of the 16th century. It is probable that a portion of the estate had been held previous to this time, as the name of "John Henryson of Fordale, serjand of the baronie of Fordale", appears in a charter of 1465. In the first half of the 15th century, Fordell belonged to Sir William de Erth (Airth) of Plean, Stirlingshire, and at his death about 1449 it was divided amongst his five daughters. In 1511 Magister James Henryson obtained from James IV a

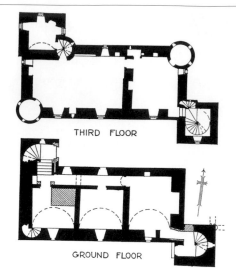

Fordell Castle – plans

charter uniting the estate into a free barony. It was the seat of George William Mercer-Henderson , and whose death it passed to his youngest sister Edith Isabella, who married in 1866 the Hon. Hamilton-Hew-Adam Duncan , second son of the 1st Earl of Camperdown.

Queen Mary is known to have visited on the occasion of the marriage of one of her Maids of Honour, Marion Scott, to George Henderson.

By the 19th century it was superseded by a newer mansion in the grounds, but it was bought and restored by Nicholas Fairbairn, Q.C. M.P.

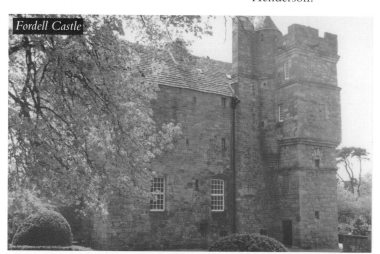

Fordell Castle

5 Commendator's House, Inchcolm

Ordnance Survey (OSR) = NT 191827

Return to the B981, and stay on that road south for 6 Km (4 miles) all the way to North Queensferry, and make your way to the Town Pier. Full sailing details are on 0131 331 4857 (24 hour information line). (Take the opportunity to visit "Deep-Sea World" - Tel: 01383 411411 for details)

Structure

In the first place, this structure, although originally a monastery, was subsequently used as a fortified castle.

There are two towers, probably built a century apart. The earlier one, of the 13th century rises two storeys above the church, is surmounted by a parapet of slight projection, carried on moulded corbels. Its windows are lancets either grouped or single.

The tower on the south side, containing the doorway and staircase to the modern house is evidently a construction of some antiquity. It retains the corbels, which carried a parapet for defence, and has apparently been the principal entrance to the abbey.

Brief History

According to Walter Bower, who was Abbot of Inchcolm and died in 1449, the monastery of St Columba of the island of Aemonia near Inverkeithing was founded about 1123

Inchcolm Abbey

by Alexander I. That king while crossing the firth at Queensferry was caught in a sudden south-westerly gale, so that he and his company, narrowly escaping with their lives, had to put into the island then called Aemonia. Accordingly he founded a monastery of Augustinian canons, additional reasons being that from his youth he had held St Columba in special veneration, further that for some years his parents had had no children until by prayers to the Saint they secured the offspring they had anxiously desired. This an odd statement because Alexander was the fifth son of Malcolm III and Queen Margaret. Alexander died in 1124. A papal bull of 1178 confirms the privileges and possessions of the priory.

In 1216 Sir Alan de Mortimer, lord of Aberdour, granted to the monks of the island of St. Columba half his lands of Aberdour, in return for the right of burial within the church for himself and his successors. This supposed accession of wealth is believed to have prompted the extension of the buildings in that century.

In 1224 Inchcolm was still only a priory, but a deed of 1233 in the Register specifies its head as an Abbot, a title which he always subsequently held.

In 1385 English invaders from a fleet plundered the church and tried to burn it. On the north side of it was a lean-to erection, which was rooted with brushwood. It was this erection, then, and not, as has been assumed, the Abbot's lodging on the first floor of the old nave and the tower that was on fire, the expectation being that the sparks would attack the roof of the church, which, however, was saved by a miraculous change of wind, brought about by the prayers to Columba of spectators on both shores of the firth.

A Lady Chapel, which was

Incholm Abbey – plan

Inchcolm Abbey

vaulted, was founded in 1402 close to the south part of the choir.

In the Act of 1581 confirming the feuing of the abbey and island to Sir James Stewart of Doune, Earl of Moray and Commendator, it is explained that at divers times the place had been seized by the English whom it served as a fortalice, while after being left waste at the Reformation it had been "receptakle to Pirates."

Open Apr-Sep
Tel: 01383 823332

6 Rosyth Castle

Ordnance Survey (OSR) = NT 108821

Back on shore, retrace your steps along the B981 (take in Deep-Sea World - 01383 411411), and take the first left towards Rosyth. The entrance to the Royal Naval Dockyard is clearly marked, but you must have prior permission from Historic Scotland (tel: 0131 668 8800) before any access can be authorised.

Structure

The existing remains are those of a rectangular enclosure of the 16th and 17th century abutting at the north-east angle on a late 15th century tower, which, though slightly altered, is complete and in much better condition than the rest of the buildings. The tower had origi-

Rosyth Castle

nally been attached to an unusually lofty barmkin, which was demolished, probably to gain light and air, when the walls of the later enclosure were erected with a series of lower structures resting against their inner sides. On the north range, however, sufficient is left to indicate that it comprised a vaulted ground floor and two upper floors and was sur-

mounted by a parapet-walk, terminating at the north-west angle in a round and at the eastern end against the tower.

The entrance is in the north range and opened into a transe, which was probably once vaulted. The gateway is set forward and may be rather later than the walling behind. In the angles of the projection are gun-loops, while other gun-loops are set in the lower part of the outer wall of the enclosure.

In the 17th century a turnpike was built against the east gable of the south range, but only portions of its foundations have survived. On the east side of the entrance is a small chamber and there are three chambers to the west, all mainly of the 16th century, but a fourth chamber on the western side of the courtyard is of the 17th century.

On the walls of the old tower there still remains traces of the original barmkin. The entrance is in the angle at the north-east corner of the courtyard. The doorway has a chamfered segmental head and is fitted for two doors, both opening inwards into a small lobby.

The hall is entered from the main staircase, and since the 17th century it has been a lofty chamber with a barrel-vaulted ceiling. In here is the inscription I.S M.N 1635, for James Stewart of Rosyth and Margaret Napier, his wife.

The main stair formerly rose from the ground to the top of the tower. On the way up, at about the level of the higher of the two entresols, there is a garderobe in the east ga-

ble, provided with
a seat and a basin
with outlet. At the
north-west angle
of the room, near
the fireplace, is a
vaulted mural
chamber, which
once gave access
to the parapet
walk of the origi-
nal barmkin. In
the north-east an-
gle is a garderobe.
In the south wall is
another mural
chamber which

Rosyth Castle

was entered from the staircase. The ceiling of
the solar has been of timber, and the side walls
bear a heavy continuous corbel-course. Above
lay a garret though now roofless.

Brief History

In 1428 the King granted and confirmed to
Sir David Stewart his barony of Rosyth,
which Stewart had resigned along with other
lands in order that the whole might be united

in one barony. Sir David is said to have been a
patron of Walter Bower, Abbot of Inchcolm.
It is said to have been the birthplace of Oliver
Cromwell's mother. Rosyth remained with
this family until the failure of male descendants towards the close of the 17th century,
when it was sold to the Earl of Rosebery, and
then passed to the Earl of Hopetoun.

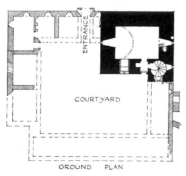
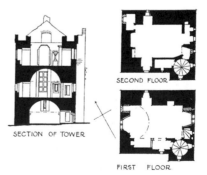

Rosyth Castle – plans and section

7 Pitreavie Castle

Ordnance Survey (OSR) = NT 117847

On exiting the Dockyard, turn left on the minor road, and then take the last exit at the next roundabout. Go straight across the next roundabout. The next roundabout is the one at the eastern end of the A823M. Immediately over the roundabout there is a right turn to Pitreavie Castle. Please enquire at the gates about access.

Structure

The original building was oblong in plan, with two wings of equal size projecting from the north side. The original entrance on the inner side of the west wing and can still be seen with the pediment above bearing the initials H.W below a star, the crest of the Wardlaws. This door was the only entrance to the building, although there was a corresponding door in the east wing leading to a blind cellar.

The roof had crow-steps on the gable walls, and dormer windows. The vaulted bottom floor contained the kitchen and a series of cellars opening off a corridor. There were no windows at this level, a defensive feature fairly common in fortified Scottish homes. Access to the upper floors was gained by two circular staircases with slits and gun holes below.

The eastern staircase has a right-handed thread ascending, while the western staircase is oppositely handed. The first floor was a series of interconnected rooms, while on the top floor, the rooms led directly off the staircase.

The house was extended and modernised in 1885 by Henry Beveridge, a wealthy mill owner. The north and west walls are probably the only original parts left. Beveridge had windows inserted in the ground floor and created bay windows in the south wall.

The sundial dating from 1644 which stood on the south lawn, was still there in 1928, but ten years later had been moved to its present site in Inveresk Lodge Garden in Musselburgh.

Brief History

In 1603, James VI acceded to the English throne, and left for London. At that time, the Scottish Court was established in Dunfermline, and the King left his palace in the care of the Queen's Chamberlain, Henry Wardlaw. In 1614, in recognition of services rendered, the King appointed Henry Wardlaw Baron of Pitreavie. A year later, Henry began the building of the castle in the grounds of his new estate.

There is anecdotal evidence that the Wardlaws sold the house to Lord Primrose, Earl of Rosebery in 1703. It is generally agreed that the house was sold in

Pittreavie

1711 to Sir Robert Blackwood, Lord Dean of Guild, Edinburgh, after which the building gradually changed from a fortified keep to an 18th century home.

The house remained in the family for 170 years, until 1884, although it lay empty for nearly a century.

The Battle of Pittreavie

In 1651, Cromwell's army found itself baulked on its way north by a Scots army which was firmly entrenched at Stirling Bridge. The armies faced each other for about a month – Cromwell, growing tired of inaction, sent a large detachment of troops under Col. Overton along the south bank of the Forth to Queensferry. It took three days for the whole army to cross, during which time the Scots army had swelled by 1000 Dunfermline men, who had marched to Inverkeithing. Battle was enjoined just east of Castlandhill (about 400 metres south of where the A90 becomes the M90) and raged for about six hours. A contingent of some 800 Highlanders arrived in time to meet the Scottish army in full retreat, and the Scottish foot-soldiers were left to face the English alone, (the cavalry having withdrawn without engaging in the battle), and they were driven back until the last remnants, some 500 strong, found themselves fighting with their backs to the wall of Pitreavie Castle. The Wardlaws sympathized with the Cromwellians "wherefore none seems to know, and showered upon the devoted warriors of the Clan Maclean stones and other missiles from the bartisans and killed them". Sir Hector, the Clan Chief and six of his sons died in the carnage. When all was over, the Wardlaws refused shelter to the wounded, and in consequence of their infamous conduct that day, it was prophesied that they never more would prosper. And so it happened – within 18 months, the first baronet died, and within 50 years the family fortunes perished and the estate sold.

Pittreavie

8 Dunfermline Palace

Ordnance Survey (OSR) = NT 089872

Dunfermline Palace

tained the King's kitchen etc. It was adjoining the latter that the connection between the monastery and the palace was situated. The kitchen contained two fireplaces and traces of vaulting. In this eastern part there was a vaulted and groined chamber supported on two octagonal pillars. This was probably used as a store house. All this part of the building is from its style, clearly ancient.

The mixture of round and pointed arches seems to point to the "transition" period from Norman to early English, or the beginning of the 13th century. The lower part of the walls of the whole south front most likely represent the work done by Bruce, and perhaps continued by his successors during the 14th century. The upper part of the south wall is in a totally different style. The large mullioned windows, with buttresses between, recall the designs of Falkland and Linlithgow, and there can be no doubt that this portion belongs to the latter half of the 15th century. The whole length of the wall is 80 metres, 18 metres high externally, but the wall of the palace next to the courtyard is only 9 metres in height.

On the level of the courtyard, and at the eastern end, was situated the hall, while the western end was occupied with another large apartment containing a large projecting oriel. This may have been the salon or withdrawing room. On the upper floors were bedrooms. All the other parts of the palace, which formed a court to the north have entirely disappeared.

Return to the road and go right on the A823 to Dunfermline. In 3 Km (2 miles), there is a large roundabout under the railway bridge. Take the first exit, and then turn right at the traffic lights, and then left just past the Carnegie Museum where car parks are signposted. In addition Abbots House, Pittencrieff House and Malcolm Canmore's Tower are all within walking distance. Details of the town of Dunfermline can be found on page 79 towards the back of this guide.

Structure

The palace is situated to the south-west of the abbey, but was connected with it by a tower through an archway, under which passes a thoroughfare to the town from the south. The palace has been greatly demolished, the only part now remaining being the south-west wall, which overlooks the ravine below and some ruins at the east end which con-

History

It was in Dunfermline that Malcolm Canmore married Margaret in 1070, the sister of Edgar Atheling, who exercised so great an influence in the introduction of civilisation and religion from the south. The Abbey of Dunfermline was founded by Malcolm and in after times one of the richest and most extensive of the monastic institutions of the country.

Here the sainted Margaret and her husband were buried, as well as a long succession of

Dunfermline Palace

kings and princes.

From Malcolm's time Dunfermline became a constant residence of the Scottish kings, and the monastery was enlarged and endowed by Alexander I and his successors. The buildings must have been of considerable extent at the time of Edward I's invasion in 1296, though whether they as yet included a Royal palace is unknown.

Edward passed some months of the winter of 1303 in Dunfermline Abbey, and on leaving set fire to and completely destroyed the buildings which had sheltered him and his army.

The abbey was restored by Robert the Bruce, and he is stated to have added a Royal palace. His son and successor, David was born here in 1323.

There does not seem to be much recorded regarding the visits of Royalty during the 15th century, but from dates of charters it is ascertained that till the time of James I, it was a frequent residence of the Kings. James IV stayed in the palace, and James V visited it during a Royal progress, with his bride, Mary of Lorraine.

Dunfermline was a principal residence of James VI, who subscribed the Solemn League and Covenant in it; and here were born David II, James I (1394) Charles I (1600), and his sister Elizabeth, Queen of Bohemia also known as the "Winter Queen" in 1596. Here, too, the "young man, Charles Stewart", kept his small court, and was kept in courteous restraint, at the time of Cromwell's invasion in 1650, and on 16 August, he subscribed the "Dunfermline Declaration", a testimony against his own father's malignancy.

Queen Anne of Denmark lived much at Dunfermline, where she had a private house of her own, which stood between the palace and the abbey church (now removed).

After the time of Charles II, the palace was allowed to fall into decay, becoming roofless in 1708.

Open daily all year except closed Thu PM and Fri Oct–Mar
Tel: 01383 739026
Make sure you visit the Abbey church: the choir is closed in winter.

9 Malcolm Canmore's Tower

Ordnance Survey (OSR) = NT 087873

> At the western end of the palace ruins is a path sign-posted Pittencrieff Park. Walk down the hill, and to the right there is an uphill climb to the ruins of Malcolm Canmore's Tower

Structure

The ruins consist of the core of the west and south walls of a rectangular structure.

It is believed to have been built between 1057 and 1070. It crowned a very steep eminence, rising abruptly from Pittencrieff Glen, and forming a peninsula, and was described as extremely strong in natural situation.

Its foundations were 20+ metres above the level of the rivulet below, but could not, from the nature of the site, have been of very great extent, probably not more than about 20 metres from east to west, and 16 metres from north to south, with a pyramidal roof.

The tower appears to have had great thickness of wall, but has been stripped to the ground of all its hewn outside stones.

History

In spite of its diminutive character, this tower was the place of Malcolm Ceannmor's marriage to the Saxon princess, St Margaret, in the spring of 1068, as well as the birthplace of "the Good Queen Maud", wife of Henry I of England. About 95 metres north-north-east of the remains is St Margarets Cave. Malcolm was first buried at Tynemouth, but afterwards taken to Dunfermline Abbey; and there in 1250 his bones were laid by his wife's when these were translated to a richly decorated shrine.

> Pittencrieff Park - the park was given as a gift to the people of Dunfermline by their famous benefactor Andrew Carnegie. As a child he had been forbidden to play in the parklands which belonged to the Lairds of Pittencrieff. In the park is the Pittencrieff House Museum (see below), which has a varied programme of Art Exhibitions, and is open from 30 April to 30 October daily except Thursdays.
>
> Nature trails, Animal and Conservation Centre, aviaries, aquaria and monkey houses are other attractions. It is a day out for all the family.

Malcolm Canmore's Tower

10 Pittencrieff House

Ordnance Survey (OSR) = NT 087873

> Continue down the path into the heart of Pittencrieff Park, and there standing proud is Pittencrieff House.

Structure

It consists of an oblong main block, lying east and west, with an oblong stair wing projecting from the middle of the south side. When built for Sir Alexander Clerk circa 1635, it was a simple laird's house of two storeys in height, but in 1731, judging from the date carved beneath the south-east skew-put, the roof was raised and another storey added. The masonry is harled, the window margins and other dressings being exposed.

The entrance, a moulded doorway, lies at the stair-foot in the west wall of the wing, and is surmounted by a little cornice. Above is a panel with enriched border, which bears a cartouche with Sir Alexander Clerk's arms and initials.

Brief History

William de Oberwill, lord of Pittencrieff, made a grant to the Abbey in 1291, and the lands apparently came into the possession of the abbots at a later date, as several tacks given by them are referred to in the 15th and 16th centuries. In 1564 John Wemyss was tacksman under the Abbey, and when the abbey lands were secularized Pittencrieff came to George Seton, 1st Earl of Dunfermline. In 1612 John Wemyss of Pittencrieff was excommunicated for the slaughter of his brother, but was received again into the Church on condition of making public profession of repentance in the kirks.

Colonel Arthur Forbes sold the estate in 1763 to Captain Archibald Grant for £11,000, and the latter disposed of it in 1787 to Captain George Phin of Southend, and then in 1799 William Hunt acquired Pittencrieff. At the end of the 19th century the laird was a major in the 79th Cameron Highlanders.

Pittencrieff House

11 *Abbot House*

Ordnance Survey (OSR) = NT 089875

> Exit the park by reversing the route through the Abbey to the town centre. Abbot House can be found on Maygate, a lower street and running parallel to the High Street. Details of the town of Dunfermline can be found on page 79, towards the back of this guide.

Structure

Two adjacent tenements, No 21 Maygate and No 11 Abbot Street are together known as Abbot House. They were built on the late 16th century and originally formed a single structure which consisted of a long rectangular main block, three main storeys in height, running east and west. It had a stair-tower projecting near the centre of the north side and another from the south-eastern angle. Turret stairs corbelled out

Abbot House

within two of the re-entrant angles gave access to chambers in the upper part of the towers. Towards the close of the 17th century there were some alteration and extension. The space on each side of the northern stair-tower was filled in and the entrance to 21 Maygate formed in the tower itself with a large lintel above it. The south-eastern stair-tower was made to serve as the abutment of a new wing.

Internal alterations made then included the removal of the vaulting in the chamber immediately opposite the new entrance and the

insertion of fireplaces there and in the kitchen adjoining. At the same time there was some reconstruction of the top storey and probably also of the dormers looking southward. Both the original house and the additions have to some extent been modernised. The final stage was its division into two.

The masonry is of rubble, harled. Most of the windows have been enlarged. Towards the garden is the south-western re-entrant angle with the stair-turret and its corbelling. In the stair wall is a small loop aligned along the main south wall. The basement-floor of the main block contained four chambers. All of them were originally vaulted, but the vaulting was in one case removed.

Brief History

It has borne witness to the intrigues of Church and State, survived fire and tempest, war and pillage and even outlasted much of the great Benedictine Abbey itself. Beneath its lovely garden lie long-forgotten graves of pilgrims and craftsmen, and below these lie abandoned medieval forges whose furnaces last glowed before Bannockburn. Within its walls Abbots and Kings have consulted on affairs of State, while great poets like Robert Henryson and Dunbar have declaimed their latest works. In

Abbot House

its time it has been an Abbot's house, a laird's mansion, an iron foundry and an art school. Forging armour for Bruce's freedom fighters, casting iron for power looms, or training pilots to fight the Luftwaffe, Abbot House has seen it all.

Abbot House Heritage Centre

This award-winning, newly renovated, tower house displays exhibits pertaining to Dunfermline's past from its Pictish origins up until the present time.

On the ground floor, which was excavated to the 15th century medieval street level, there is the Servery (scene outside the house looking across 15th to 16th Maygate); Café (West vault was an iron foundry and the east vault was a bakery); Shop (Both vaults formed the kitchen) and Fire Room which depicts the scene outside the house in May 1624 during the Great Fire of Dunfermline.

The first floor has the following attractions :-
Passage – The Picts in Fife.
St Margaret Room – Religious history of Dunfermline 1066 to 1560.
Lady Halkett's Room – This room replaced the wooden gallery lost in the Great Fire in 1624.
Presence Chamber – Has a traceried win-

dow, dated 1450-60 and built into the original front wall of the house. There is also part of an original 16th century mural in this room.
Marbled Chamber – Decorated in the 17th century style. Display cases show replicas of the Pitfirrane Goblet from which James VI drank his farewell to Dunfermline before going south in 1603.
Reform Room – 18th century living room with figures of Skirving and Mealmaker, prominent members of Friends of the People Movement, who were transported to Australia.
East Landing – Cast of the Annunciation Stone, a medieval carved stone found in the window of a room in Dunfermline's Royal Palace.
War Room – Dining room of the late 18th/ 19th century extension.

Similarly on the second floor :-
Industry Room – Lost industries of Dunfermline.
Long Gallery – Historical Thistle Tree mural on ceiling showing history of Dunfermline from 9th to 20th century.
Entertainment Room – Art Deco background to the story of cinema, theatre and music.
1964 Room – Decorated as living-room and café of the 1960s.

For information – 01383 733266

12 Hill House

Ordnance Survey (OSR) = NT 092860

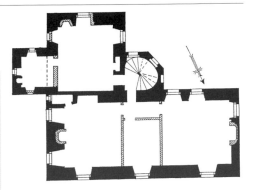

From the car park behind the Andrew Carnegie Birthplace Museum, return down the hill to the traffic lights. Turn right and then first left on Forth Street/Limekilns Road. Shortly after passing over the railway line take the first left, and Hill House is a few hundred metres on the left.

Hill House – plan

Structure

Hill House is a 17th century house which consists of an oblong main block running roughly east and west. There is a wing projecting southward in alignment with the eastern gable, and a stair tower within the re-entrant angle, and a second tower which projects eastward from the wing, although it is contemporary with the other parts. The front is faced with ashlar, the sides and back are built of rubble. The front windows and those of the east tower have architraves enriched with a roll-and-hollow moulding of a type common in Fife from the close of the 16th century.

The ground floor is not vaulted. The first floor contained the principal apartments, all of which are modernised. Above the south wing and east tower is an attic floor reached by a small stair on the mid-wall, which also gave access to a tiny chamber above the main staircase.

Brief History

The initials W. M. surmounted by the fleur-de lys appear to be those of William Monteith of Randieford, who acquired the lands of Hill in 1621, and obtained a charter for them in 1624, and who, it may be presumed, erected this mansion in 1623, the date below the front window. He was an elder in this parish in 1640.

Hill House

13 Pitfirrane

Ordnance Survey (OSR) = NT 060863

Return to the A906 and turn left. After 2 Km (1.25 miles) turn right on the A985. In 1 Km (0.7 miles) turn right on an unmarked road to Crossford, which meets the A994 after 2 km (1.25 miles). Turn left and very shortly there is a left turn into Pitfirrane Golf Club. Pitfirrane Castle is the Club House.

Structure

It was a composite structure, the oldest part of which was not earlier than the 15th century, when the lands belonged to the family of Halket. The 15th century tower was an oblong tower, and contained a ground floor

Pitfirrane Castle

with a vaulted entresol above it and at least two upper floors. On each floor there appeared to have been two chambers, the western ones being the smaller. The entrance lay in the south wall and opened into a small lobby giving direct access to the larger ground floor chamber and to two mural stairs which rose to the first floor; from the western of these the entresol level was reached.

In 1583 the wall-head was removed, and the tower heightened by the addition of a storey with turrets corbelled out at its western angles. A new wing was also built, projecting southwards in alignment with the west gable. It contained a spacious newel stair approached from the west and ascending to the second floor, above which were chambers reached from a turret-stair corbelled out within the re-entrant angle, the lowest member of the corbelling representing a grotesque head. Above the new entrance thus provided there was placed an armorial panel, which had a chamfered margin enriched with roses, and bears on the lintel, in raised figures, the date 1583.

Three piles conjoined in point, on a chief a lion passant, for Halket. Above was a label with the motto, FIDES SVFICIT. Higher up on the same wall was a double coat of arms, and in its upper part are the Royal Arms of Scotland with supporters, and in its lower part the arms of Halket, impaling Hepburn. On a chevron was a rose between two lions combatant, and in base three martlets two and one. The dexter supporter is a falcon jessed and belled, and the sinister a unicorn. The helm is mantled and the crest is that of Halket, while above it, on a label, are the mottoes of the two families. Below the shield are the initials G. H. and I. H., for George Halket and Isabel Hepburn of Waughton.

The 16th century work is in fine ashlar, and the windows have a quirked edge-roll wrought on jambs and lintels.

Brief History

It was the seat of Sir Peter Arthur Halket of

Pitfirrane and was in the possession of that family since the beginning of the 15th century. The first of the family was David de Halkett, who was the proprietor of the lands of Ballingal in the time of David II, and his grandson, who bore the same name, was designated of Petfurane in a charter of 1437.

Pittfirrane Castle at the end of the 19th century

Through the marriage of one of the Halketts with a daughter of Kinninmond of Craighall the superiority of a third part of Pitfirrane passed into the hands of that family; and the Scotts of Craighall acquired this right and exercised it. Of the sons of George Halkett, who succeeded the estate in 1573, the elder, Robert, succeeded him, and was knighted by James VI, and the younger, John, who represented Kirkcaldy in the Parliament of 1593, received a similar honour, was colonel of a Scots regiment in the army of the States of Holland, and fell at the siege of Bois-le-duc in 1628. Sir Robert's son, Sir James, was colonel of horse in the army of the Covenanters, and was MP for Fifeshire in 1649. Sir Charles Halkett, son of Sir James was created a baronet of Nova Scotia in 1662, and represented Dunfermline at the Convention of 1689, whereby the Revolution settlement was effected. He died in 1697. His son James was provost of Dunfermline and MP for that burgh from 1702 till his death in 1705. As he was unmarried the baronetcy expired, but the estates fell to his sister Janet, who had married Sir Peter Wedderburn of Gosford, a descendant of the Wedderburns of Blackness, near Dundee. Sir Peter assumed the name of Halkett, and as he had been created a baronet in 1697 his descendants continued the title styling themselves "of Pitfirrane" instead "of Gosford". He succeeded his brother-in-law, and sat in the first Parliament of Great Britain. He died in 1746. His eldest son, Sir Peter, was member for the Stirling Burghs in 1734-41, and was a distinguished officer on the Hanoverian side during the Jacobite Rebellion of 1745. He was taken prisoner at Gladsmuir by the troops of Prince Charles Edward, and was released on parole; and afterwards refused to rejoin his regiment when ordered by the Duke of Cumberland to do so, preferring to forfeit his commission rather than break his parole. His determination in this respect was affirmed by Parliament, and in 1754 he embarked for America as colonel of the 44th Regiment, and fell in battle at Monongahela in 1755. His youngest son James was slain in the same engagement; his second son Francis, major in the Black Watch, died in 1760; and thus when his eldest son Sir Peter died unmarried in 1779, the title went to Sir John Wedderburn of Gosford. The latest additions to Pitfirrane were carried out at the end of the 19th century by the eighth baronet, Sir Arthur Halkett.

14 *Culross Palace*

Ordnance Survey (OSR) = NS 986862

Return to the A994 and turn left. Travel for 3 Km (2 miles), and at the roundabout go straight across on the B9037. Culross Palace is a further 5.5 Km (3.5 miles) in Culross. Details of the town of Culross can be found on page 81, near the end of this guide.

Structure

The house, which is sometimes called "the Colonel's Close", was built between 1597 and 1611 by George Bruce of Culross, later of

Culross Palace

Carnock. It has grown in stages, the oldest part being the central wing on the west side of the outer courtyard. In the early 17th century there was a radical reconstruction. On the north an extension was erected, housing a turnpike and providing additional offices on the lower floor, while a long gallery, the northern end of which covered part of the original structure, was run out towards the south. A further addition which can be dated to 1611, is the large isolated block on the north of the outer courtyard. The last addi-

tion was a wing thrown out on the north side of the oldest part beside the turnpike.

The outer courtyard was entered from the south between a pair of modest 17th century piers.

Immediately beyond the landing lay what was the original house, three-storeyed and rubble built. There is nothing to show how admission was had to the ground floor of the original house. After reconstruction it was entered from the inner court on the north and also from a door set at the southern end of a passage which ran through its centre.

History

Sir George Bruce was a commercial magnate of the time. Third son of Edward Bruce of Blairhall, he engaged in commerce and worked collieries and salt-pans to such profit that he was enabled to acquire the estate of Carnock, embracing the greater part of the parishes of Culross and Carnock. He was knighted by James VI and died in 1625. The 1st and 2nd Earls of Kincardine, Bruce's grandson and great-grandson, occupied the house, but about 1700 it passed by judicial sale to Colonel John Erskine of Carnock, popularly called "the Black Colonel"

The Palace is managed by The National Trust for Scotland. It is open to the public from April to September.
Tel: 01383 880359.

15 Dunimarle Castle

Ordnance Survey (OSR) = NS 978859

Dunimarle

Brief History

It was said to be where Lady Macduff and her children were murdered by order of Macbeth, but this has questionable authenticity.

The estate was formerly called Castlehill and was for centuries in the possession of the Blairs, who intermarried with the Elgin and Rosebery families. The Blairs disposed of the property to Lady Kirk of Tulliallan, who in turn sold it to Miss Erskine. She made many alterations on the property and restored it to the original name of Dunimarle. She married Admiral Sharp, and died in the spring of 1872. By her will, she left all her property to trustees.

The present castle, an extension of the 18th century mansion house, was an art museum until its poor state of repair forced its closure. It did contain priceless antiques including furniture owned by Napoleon.

The trustees, which included Lord Wemyss, were determined to save the place, and successfully approached the Historic Buildings Council.

Continue westwards on the B9037, and the newer Dunimarle Castle can be seen from the road after 1 Km (0.6 miles). Contact should be made with the occupants to view the ruins of the original castle.

Structure

To the west of the present mansion are the ruins of an earlier house built against a wall which may have been part of the medieval Dunimarle Castle. At its northern end are the remains of a domical-vaulted structure, thought to be the ground floor of a tower.

The new castle of 1839-45 incorporates a small late 18th century mansion house. It is dominated by a projecting four-storey tower under a machicolated parapet. There are continuous corbelled and crenellated balcony under the first-floor windows and individual stone balconies under the upper windows.

The castles and grounds are not open to the public. Stuart Fisher and his family occupy the building, and a polite request to view may be rewarded. He has diligently restored parts of the grounds, especially the King's Walk, which he has transformed from a jungle.

16 *Tulliallan Castle*

Ordnance Survey (OSR) = NS 927888

Continue on the B9037 for 5 Km (3 miles) and then turn right on the A876 into Kincardine. At the roundabout, take the first left on the A977 to Alloa. There is a left turn after 700 metres into the entrance, opposite the Police College. To gain entrance please ring the caretaker beforehand on 01259 731401 for permission.

Structure

It is of special interest, as it has features of arrangement and detail unique in Scottish architecture. It stands within an enclosure, roughly D-shaped and girt with a broad ditch

Tulliallan Castle

having a rampart outside of it, the chord of the arc being on the north.

The castle is not wholly of one time, and the date and extent of the earliest work in it are in some doubt. It consists of an oblong main block, facing south and running roughly east and west, three-storeyed at one end and

four-storeyed at the other, while two wings which have obviously been added to it, project from its northern wall in alignment with the gables. At its south-western angle is a tower which projects only slightly on the south, but develops into a semi-octagon on the west. This contains the principal staircase. A semi-hexagon in which there is a service stair, is placed midway along the western wall, masking what may once have been the north-west corner. The ground floor of the main block, with the lower part of the south-west tower and of the two staircases, is not unlike 14th century architecture.

There are two entrances on the south, the principal one in the south-west tower, and the other at the east end of the main block. The former was protected by a portcullis and a barred door, while a mound in front of it may be the foundations of a detached structure on which the outer end of a drawbridge rested when lowered. The entrance at the east end, which opened directly into what must have been the old hall, had also a drawbridge, as well as two doors with bars. A third entrance at the north-west corner gives admission from the west wing, but was apparently designed to be external as it had two barred doors.

For the greater part of its length beginning from the eastern corner, the facade presents a view of two storeys and an attic, the floor of the attic being just beneath the wall-head. But as the re-entrant angle formed by the south-west tower was approached, the wall-head rose and the attic became a third storey. About the middle of the tower it rose again to form the front of the cap-house, from which a higher parapet-walk was reached. On the first floor besides a slit in the wall of the tower, designed to light the staircase, there were two great windows on the south with chamfered jambs and lintels. These were enlarged, apparently in the 16th or 17th century. The attic was lit by small windows which could be seen between the lower corbels and which must have been at its floor level, a quite abnormal arrangement.

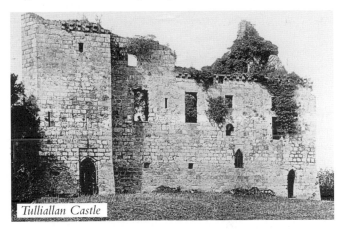

Tulliallan Castle

On the north the upper portion of the walls of the west wing and of the main block had disappeared.

Towards the junction of the latter with the east wing, part of the wall-head remained with a few of the corbels of the parapet, while the east wing itself was nearly complete. Its uppermost storey was intaken on the gable, and the skew is crow-stepped. The gables of the wings contained garderobe shoots, the eastern one discharging below the ground level, while the outlet for that on the west was marked by a cutting back of the rock.

The oldest masonry, that of the main block, extended from the south-east corner as far as a buttress-like projection which masked the north-east corner as it was before the wing was added. The corbels for the original parapet passed above the buttress and the line was continued as far as the north-east corner by the broken remains of others, apparently later and designed to support the parapet of the second period. In the third period the wing was given an additional storey and crowned by a crow-stepped cap-house, the highest part of the whole structure, both of those being

reached by a turnpike which rose from the first floor.

The principal entrance to the castle was that in the south-west tower. Beyond the foot of the staircase, which was on the left, a door once provided with a bar, admitted directly to the ground floor of the main block. This was originally divided into two chambers of unequal length.

Brief History

In 1304 Edward I was ordering his sheriff of Clackmannan to strengthen the walls of "Tolyalwyn". The lands of Tulliallan with the fortalice were granted in 1410 by Archibald, Earl of Douglas, to Sir John Edminstone. The Edminstone line ended in two daughters, and, in the spring of 1485-6, Elizabeth Edminstone, wife of Patrick Blackadder, exchanged with her sister certain lands in Banff for the latter's share of the lands of Tulliallan. Thereafter the whole lands were conferred upon John Blackadder, the son, and continued with this family till the beginning of the 17th century. After 1605 they were found in the hands of Sir George Bruce of Carnock. In 1619 five men under trial for the incarceration of another in the "pitt of Tullieallane, quhair, throw want of intertenement, he famischet and deit of hunger".

17 Bordie Castle

Ordnance Survey (OSR) = NS 956869

Return to the A977 and turn right, back into Kincardine. At the roundabout, take the first left on the A985. In 2.5 Km (1.5 miles), Bordie Castle is on your right within a farm complex.

Structure

It is said to be nothing more than an abortive work which was never completed, but the other view is that it is the remains of an L-shaped house of the 17th century, which has been three storeys and an attic in height. The part still standing has evidently been the wing, while on the west can be traced a fragment of the west gable of the main block, containing one jamb of the entrance. In the east wall is one small window which has back-set margins and a triangular pediment.

Brief History

Three hundred metres due north is the Standard Stone in which the Scottish Standard was fixed on the occasion of the battle of Culross which in the 11th century saw Duncan's army face the invading Danes.

Bordie Castle

18 Killernie Castle

Ordnance Survey (OSR) = NT 032924

Continue on the A985 for 4 Km (2.5 miles), then turn left on the B9037. It is 3 Km (2 miles) before the junction with the A907. Turn right and travel eastwards for 5 Km (3.25 miles) through the village of Oakley. Turn left on the B913 to Saline. The village is a further 3.5 Km (2.5 miles). Turn right on the B914 and the ruins can be seen almost immediately on the left, nestled against the hillside.

Structure

The remains of this building stand at the western edge of a small plateau, backed by rising ground. Although the structure is mainly represented by foundations, sufficient is left to indicate that it has been a tower of the late 16th century (1592), oblong on plan but having circular towers projecting from the north-western and south-eastern angles. The western tower is ruinous, standing only to the height of the vault which covers its ground floor. The eastern tower has contained a newel stair. Its wall is very incomplete, but at one point is still standing 15 feet high. Only the three lowest steps of the stair remain. This tower also has had gun-loops. On the south side of the castle there appears to have been an enclosure, heavily revetted on the western side, where the ground falls.

Brief History

In 1542 Killernie was among the lands held on lease by Sir James Colville of East Wemyss but forfeited by him and conferred on Robert Dury of that ilk. The estate on which the castle stood belonged formerly to one Scot of Balneiry (= Balweary).

Killernie Castle

19 Knockdavie Castle

Ordnance Survey (OSR) = NT 213883

It is a long way to Knockdavie. Continue on the B914/A909 for 12 Km (7.5 miles), until the junction with the B996. Turn right and stay on the A909 through Cowdenbeath for 6 Km (4 miles) to the junction with the B9157. Turn left and inside 2 Km (1.25 miles) Knockdavie can be seen on the hillside to the right.

Structure

It has been a small 17th century T-plan house, oblong on plan, lying east and west with rubble built walls. On the north is a semi-circular projection for a turnpike-stair.

Brief History

It is said to have belonged to a Douglas in the 17th century, known as an opponent of the Covenanters.

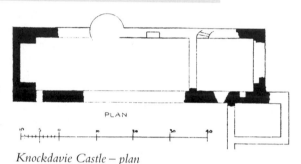

PLAN

Knockdavie Castle – plan

Knockdavie Castle

20 Balmuto Tower

Ordnance Survey (OSR) = NT 221898

Continue on the A907 for 1 Km (0.625 miles) and the entrance is on the left. Under no circumstance should you enter without prior permission from the owners.

Balmuto Tower

Structure

The mansion of Balmuto included a 15th century tower, two 16th century additions, and sundry modern extensions. The tower was best seen from the north. It is oblong in plan and contained three storeys beneath the wall-head, the lowest being vaulted. The masonry was of coursed rubble. The wall-head was surmounted by a cavetto cornice enriched with small corbels.

On the south side of the tower there were two entrances. The lower one, which had been considerably restored, opened into a small mural lobby giving access on the north to the ground floor and on the east to a mural staircase. The upper entrance, which led directly to the first floor, was widened in the 16th century, but finally blocked up in the 17th.

Of the earlier additions, that on the west immediately adjoining the tower, consisted of a vaulted ground-floor and two upper storeys. That on the south, parallel to the tower, consisted of a ground floor, vaulted except at the eastern end where there has been an alteration, and of an upper floor.

The lintel on the doorway bears a panel inscribed I.B.I.S. 1594 for John Boswell and his wife Isabella Sandilands.

Brief History

Sir John Boswell, who succeeded in 1582, was a favourite at the Court of James VI, and in a special charter dated 1587 it is expressly stated that the castle of Balmuto had been destroyed in his minority. The estate remained in this branch of the family till 1722, when Andrew Boswell sold Balmuto to John Boswell, a cadet of the Boswells of Auchinleck in Ayrshire, who was descended from a junior branch of the Boswells of Balmuto. This John Boswell was the uncle of Loch Auchinleck of Session, and consequently grand-uncle of James Boswell, the biographer of Doctor Johnson. His son was Claude Balmuto, Lord Balmuto of Session, who died in 1824.

21 Rossend Castle

Ordnance Survey (OSR) = NT 225859

Return to the A907 and turn right, re-tracing your steps for 3 Km (1.75 miles), passing Knockdavie. Turn left on A909 to Burntisland which is 5 Km (3.25 miles) away. Park wherever possible in the town, and head for the High Street. Sailors Seaforth is a western extension of the High Street, and Rossend Castle can be seen there.

Rossend Castle

Structure

The castle is a 16th century house, extended, modernised and still occupied. The original house was L-shaped on plan and now forms the eastern part of the whole structure. The main block ran north and south and had two chambers in its length. A short wing, projecting westward in alignment with the main north gable, contained a turnpike on its lower floors and a chamber in its upper part. This type of plan is believed to have originated about the middle of the 16th century.

The original re-entrant angle was filled in early in the 17th century, with a long wing running westward from the main block and rectangular to it, but in alignment with the south wall of the original wing; the northern re-entrant, formed by the two wings, has been closed by a modern addition.

The original house and its extension are four storeys in height.

Brief History

The land at one time belonged to the Abbey of Dunfermline, but in 1552 the Commendator of the Abbey (Abbot George Dury of Durie) granted to Peter Dury the lands of "the nether grange of Kinghorne Wester called the Mains with the custody of the fortalice." This post carried with it "the lands of Greiflandis and Cwnyngerlandis now called Brunteland," and the previous occupant was Robert Dury of that ilk. Later the property was in the hands of Sir Robert Melville of Murdocairnie, who lost it through forfeiture, after which it was conferred in 1571 on David Dury of that ilk, including "the manor, tower, and fortalice of Bryntyland with the houses, buildings and gardens." Subsequently however, these lands were once again in possession of the Melvilles of Murdocairnie, from they passed to Sir James Wemyss of Caskiebirran, created Lord Burntisland for life in 1672.

Queen Mary stayed there in 1563, hence the name of the southern chamber

Currently it is the offices of a firm of architects L.A.Rolland & Hurd Partners, and therefore any request to view should be directed to the occupants

Directions to Aberdour Castle (No 1) page 41

Return northwards out of Burntisland to the A921 and go westwards. Aberdour is 6 Km (3.75 miles) away.

Castle Touring Guides

Additional Information

Index of Castles

Falkland

Falkland is a small royal burgh (blessed by James II in 1458) and lies at the foot of the East Lomond Hill. Its character derives mainly

was ideal for hawking as well as hunting deer and wild boar.

Falkland prospered due to the spinning and weaving of flax which developed into a thriving cottage industry. Eventually mechanisa-

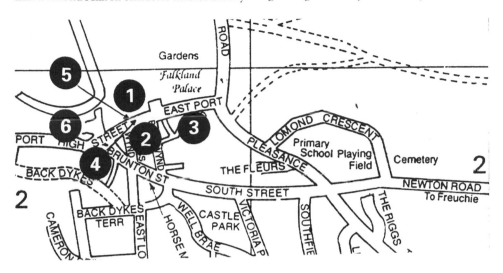

from its associations with the Stewart kings who built the attractive palace that dominates the High Street, and frequented it as a hunting lodge. The Stewarts ruled Scotland for more than two centuries before the union with the English crown.

Like all royal burghs it could now have a Mercat Cross, which was a prized medieval symbol of the right to trade, and it was empowered to hold weekly markets and to have annual fairs at the time of the Feast of All Saints.

It rose in importance in the 14th century when the Stewart monarchy acquired Falkland Castle from Macduff, the Thane of Fife. Unlike the Picts who had built a fort on the East Lomond for defensive purposes the Stewarts were interested in Falkland as a place of sport, relaxation and entertainment. The name of Falkland is associated with falconry which was one of the popular sports in the area and the Howe of Fife with its vast forests

tion and the building of linen factories had replaced the handloom weaver by the early 19th century. The factory at the Pleasance in Falkland continued to produce linen until 1974.

Standing in the shadows of the parish church is the bronze statue of Onesiphorus Tyndall-Bruce who, along with his wife Margaret contributed so much to the village. They had inherited the Nuthill Estates at Falkland and in 1839 commissioned architect William Burn to design the House of Falkland as their home. When that was complete they financed the restoration of the parish church and later built the Bruce Fountain which stands in the village square.

It is now a conservation area and on a walk through the streets you can see the features that make the village attractive.

General Information

No Tourist Information Centre. Half day closing – Thursday.

Falkland Hill Race and Falkland Festival in June. In summer months various musical events in Falkland Palace and Gardens.

"A Falkland Guide" by the Falkland Society is available in most retail outlets in the town.

Local Attractions (see the map above)
1. **Parish Church**- Gothic (built 1849/50) stands on the site of a church built in 1620 by John Mylne.
2. **Town Hall-** Bought by the NTS. Stag under the Oak Tree crest on the pediment.
3. **Moncrieff House**-17th house with the only intact thatched roof. Marriage lintel over the door.
4. **Mercat Cross** - Only the shape of a cross in cobbles now recalls the proud symbol of the right to trade.

5. **Bruce Fountain –** Tyndall Bruce gift. lions display coat of arms and the Burgh crest.
6. **Weavers Cottage** - restored by the NTS. Typical home and work-shop of the early handloom weavers.

Where to Eat
Hayloft Tea Rooms, Back Wynd
Kind Kyttocks Kitchen
Zoie's, High Street

Accommodation
Covenanter Hotel, High Street
The Hunting Lodge Hotel, High Street
Lomond Hills Hotel, High Street, Freuchie
Malt Barn Inn, Main Street, Newton of Falkland
Lomond Tavern, Horsemarket Street

Falkland Palace

Dysart

General Information

This is a place of antiquity, its history beginning with the half mythical St Serf, who is said to have held his famous discussion with Satan in a cave in Lord Rosslyn's grounds

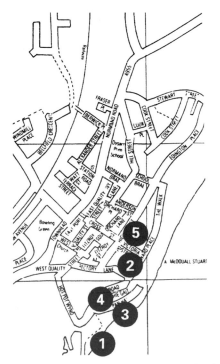

above the Old Church, and whose cell, the said cave (Lat. *Desertum,* a solitude) is supposed to have given it its name.

Mid 15th century Dysart was a burgh of barony, till early in the 16th it was raised to a royal burgh by James V.

Local Attractions (see the map above)

1. **Harbour**- Formerly a busy port for tall ships bringing wine, pantiles and general cargos from the Netherlands, and taking away coal, salt etc.

2. **John McDouall Stuart Museum**- Born in Rectory Lane, his 17th century birthplace has been incorporated into a museum depicting the explorer's life. In 1861-2 he was the first man to cross Australia from the southern coast to the north through the central desert.

3. **Pan Ha'**- These white 17th and 18th century fisher houses take their name from the ancient salt pans nearby. Restored by the National Trust for Scotland. No.11 was the Shoremaster's House, No.10 the Pilot's House, No.9 the Tide-Waiter's House, No.8 the Covenant House and No.7 the Girnal.

4. **St Serf's Tower**- Remains of possibly the finest example in Scotland of a battlemented church tower. It is the nave and saddle-roofed tower of the ruinous kirk, second pointed in style, and therefore a good deal earlier than the date 1570 on one of its mullionless windows.

5. **Tolbooth**- Of 1576.

St Serf's, Dysart

Kirkcaldy

General Information

At one time known as the "Lang Toun", Kirkcaldy is the main shopping centre of the Kingdom. It is home of the famous "Links

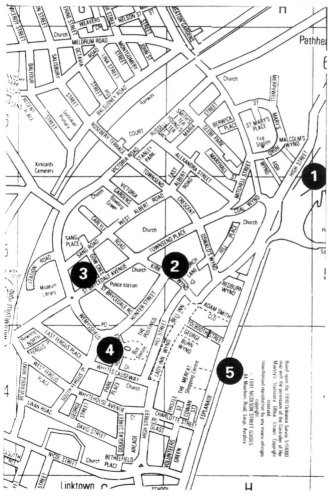

majestic 15th century castle, is a favourite spot for picnics.

Local Attractions (see the map)

1. **Ravenscraig Castle** – see comprehensive details in the main body of the guide

2. **Kirk Wynd** – a number of old buildings are to be found, among them St Brycedale Church and Kirkcaldy's Old Kirk with its Norman tower. It was consecrated by the Bishop of St Andrews in 1244. It has famous stained glass windows, including those by Burne-Jones and William Morris. There is one of the earliest portrait paintings in Scotland, that of the Rev George Gillespie, who was a former General Assembly Moderator and a member of the Westminster Assembly.

3. **Adam Smith Theatre** – named after the founder of the science of political economy who was born in the town. Information on 01592 202855.

4. **Town House** – building commenced in 1939 as a result of an architectural competition. A mural decorating the stairwell is a pictorial history of Kirkcaldy as depicted by artist Walter Pritchard. A feature adjacent to the Town House is the collection of six lamps representing burghs which have ceased to exist as from 1975.

Market", reputed to be the largest street fair in Britain. Many parks and gardens can be found in and around Kirkcaldy, and near the town centre lies the Beveridge Park with tree-lined walks, boating lake and pets corner, while the Ravenscraig Park, with the nearby

5. **Links Market** – reputed to be the longest street fair in Britain and taked place every April on the Esplanade

76

Kirkcaldy

Tourist Information Centre
19 Whytecauseway, Kirkcaldy KY1 1XF – 01592 267775

Accommodation
Hotels
Dean Park Hotel, Chapel Level – 01592 261635
Dunniker House Hotel, Dunniker Park, Dunniker Way – 01592 268393
Parkway Hotel, Abbotshall Road – 01592 292143
Royal Hotel, Townhead, Dysart – 01592 654112
Streathean Hotel, 2 Wishart Place, Dysart Road – 01592 652210
Victoria Hotel, 28 Victoria Road – 01592 260117

Bed and Breakfast
Adelly, 56 Loughborough Road – 01592 652576
Bennochy Bank Guest House, 26 Carlyle Road – 01592 200733
Cameron House, 44 Glebe Park – 01592 264531
Cherrydene, 44 Bennochy Road – 01592 202147
Castleview, 17 Dysart Road – 01592 269275
Crawford Hall, 2 Kinghorn Road – 01592 262568

Dunedin House, 25 Townsend Place – 01592 269588
Elmsmere, 49 Townsend Place – 01592 269588
Invertiel Guest House, 21 Pratt Street – 01592 264849/640103
Norview, 59 Normand Street – 01592 652804
Lubelle Guest House, 19 Bennochy Road – 01592 205932
Northhall Guest House, 143 Victoria Street – 01592 268864
Pitteadie House – 01592 260632
Richmond, 34 Victoria Road – 01592 261258
Rowan Cottage, 5 Melrose Crescent – 01592 267305
Scotties B&B, 213 Nicol Street – 01592 268596
Wemysshof, 69 Lady Nairn Avenue – 01592 652806

Other Facilities
Kirkcaldy Museum and Art Gallery, War Memorial Gardens
Citizens Advice Bureau, 11 Wemyssfield – 01592 264021
Kirkcaldy Golf Club, Balwearie Road – 01592 205240

Lochore Meadows Country Park

PARK MAP

Countryside for everyone

Key

— · — · — Wheelchair accessible path	▨ Trees
— — — Well-marked path	☐ Site of special interest
• • • • • • Indistinct path	P Car Park
▬▬▬ Country Park boundary	
⁄⁄⁄⁄⁄ No through road	Approx. scale = 1/2 mile

General Information

The country park is an attractive area of re-claimed coal-mining waste land. It is open throughout the year.

Fishing. Horse riding. Orienteering. Golf and putting. Windsurfing. Adventurous Play Area, beach, picnics, barbecues
Wheelchair access
Information tel: 01592 414300

Dunfermline

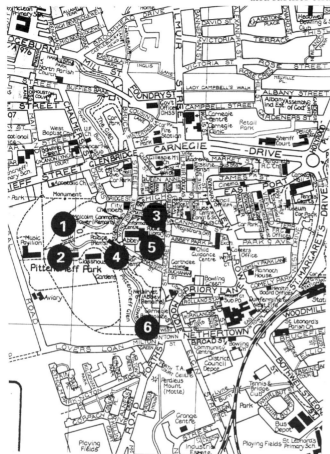

was endowed both by that king and by his sons Ethelred and Eadgar, and was completed and further endowed by Alexander I in 1115. Remodelled in 1124 as a Benedictine Abbey by David I, who placed in it an abbot and twelve brethren brought from Canterbury, it had become by the close of the 13th century one of the most extensive and magnificent monastic establishments in Scotland. It was occupied by Edward I of England for six months from November 1303, and by him was set on fire. It was restored under Bruce, but in 1560 it was "cast down" by the Reformers. The nave alone was spared and this was refitted in 1564 and again at the end of the century.

6. Andrew Carnegie Birthplace Museum – Moodie Street. 01383 724302. The Birthplace Museum traces the life story of the emigrant weaver's son who became the richest man in the world. As the steel king of America, he forged a fortune in the furnaces of Pittsburgh – and spent the rest of his life giving it away for the benefit of others.

Local Attractions (see the map above)

1. **Malcolm Canmore's Tower** – The ruins are covered in detail within the guide.
2. **Pittencrieff House** – The House and park are covered in detail within the guide.
3. **Abbot House** – The House is covered in detail within the guide.
4. **Dunfermline Palace** – The Palace is covered in detail within the guide.
5. **Dunfermline Abbey** – The Abbey originated in the founding in 1072 of the church of the Holy Trinity by Malcolm Canmore. It

Tourist Information Centre

13 Maygate, Dunfermline – 01383 720999

Accommodation

Hotels

Pitbauchlie House Hotel, Aberdour Road RAC★★★ and AA ★★★ (01383 722282)

Abbey Park Hotel, 5 Abbey Park Place (01383 739686)
Auld Toll Tavern, 121 St. Leonard's Street (01383 721489)
Brucefield Manor Hotel, Woodmill Road (01383 722199)

Bed & Breakfast
Clark Cottage Guest House, 139 Hallbeath Road (01383 735935)
The Haven, 82 Pilmuir Street (01383 729039)
Hopetoun Lodge, 141 Hallbeath Road (01383 620906)
House of Gask, Lathalmond (01383 839761)

Pubs & Inns
Cottage Inn, 140 Hospital Hill (01383 737784)
Coady's, 16 Pilmuir Street (01383 723865)
The Elizabethan, Halbeath Road (01383 725877)
Jinty's, 6-8 Netherton Broad St. (01383 725806)
Cask Bar, 18 Bridge Street (01383 722538)
East Port Bar, East Port (01383 736678)
Old Inn, 13 Kirkgate (01383 736652)

Dunfermline

Carnegie Museum, Dunfermline

Culross

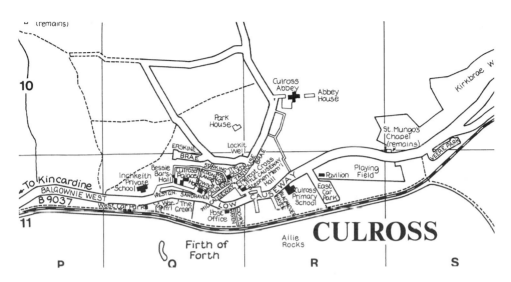

CULROSS

Introduction

Malcolm, Earl of Fife founded a religious house at Culross in 1217. Before that, as early as the 6th century, there was an important religious centre here, with Culross said to be the birthplace of St Mungo, patron saint of Glasgow and founder of its cathedral. The monks were also the first miners, as they were in order communities founded on the once plentiful coal of the Lothians and Forth Valley. By the 16th century there were extensive, though mainly shallow, workings in the area around Culross.

Local Attractions (see the map above)

Culross Palace - The Palace is covered in detail within the guide.

Culross Abbey - Founded in 1217 by Malcolm, the 7th Earl of Fife. It was dedicated to St Mary and St Serf.

The Town House - it is now used as the National Trust for Scotland Visitors Centre which contains an exhibition and video. Built in 1625 its architecture has a strong Flemish influence.

The Mercat Cross - Originally made from one piece of stone in 1588, it was restored in 1902 by Sir James Sievwright.

Culross

Culross Abbey

Accommodation
Hotel
Dundonald Arms Hotel, Mid Causeway (01383 881137)

Bed & Breakfast
Woodhead Farm (01383 880270)
Harveston, Low Causeway (01383 881830)
St Mungos Cottage, Low Causeway (01383 882102)
Langlees Farm, Newmills (01383 881152)
The Cottage, Blairburn (01383 880704)
The Old Manse, 136 Main Street, Newmills (01383 880150)

Culross - Town House

The Scottish Castles Associations

At the launch of the first Fife Castles guide book at Fernie Castle, the Laird of Balgonie and Eddergoll, was trying to persuade his colleagues to form an association of castle

SCA inaugural meeting – 24th June 1996

owners. His efforts were fruitless, mainly through a lack of available time. I thought about it for a few days, and then wrote to the Laird offering administrative help.

From a mail shot of around 350 to what was believed to be occupied castles in February 1996, there were some 70 responses, not all of which were positive. Nevertheless there was a core of owners who wished to pursue the possibility of an organisation. Eventually an initial meeting was held at Culcreuch Castle in Stirlingshire, and attended by seven owners (Plane, Wormistone, Lochhouse, Culcreuch, Kelly, Balgonie and Strathendry).

For the next 18 months, membership grew gradually as, in parallel, the Association defined its constitution, aims and objectives etc.,

and also organised its first castle visit weekend, in Fife, coupled with its first AGM, at Balgonie Castle. Further visits were held in June (East Lothian) and September (Aberdeenshire), before a crucial "Way Forward" workshop at Culcreuch Castle.

Pivotal to the organisation's short term success was to build on and formalise its Castle Visits Programme, which gives access to those castles not open to the public. Developing a three-year schedule, 1998 consisted of weekends in Dumfries and Caithness & the Orkneys plus a day in the Borders. Lothian was revisited in February 1999, with Perthshire (April), Fife/Dundee (June), Ireland (September) and Ayrshire in November to follow.

Its first Conference was well attended in September 1998, and had several distinguished speakers (Nigel Tranter - the President, Prof Charles McKean, Dr Chris Tabraham, Dr Aonghus McKenzie, Dr Michael Bath and Judy, Lady Steel of Aikwood.)

Another key attraction is its Newsletter, where the Editor, John Buchanan Smith, has delivered an excellent and readable product. Growing in statue his castle drawings are a prominent feature.

Exceeding 100 members which includes over 65 castle owners, the organisation is rapidly moving forward, and further details of it including membership can be found on the next page.

The Association seeks to achieve its objectives by :-
• Improving the public's awareness of Scot-

tish castles as a valuable inheritance and tangible reminder of its cultural heritage

- Attracting as wide a membership as possible, encompassing castle owners, keepers and carers; potential owners and restorers; architects, artists and craftsmen; academics, students, writers and historians; and enthusiastic members of the general public
- Providing a forum for interested individuals and organisations to discuss issues of common concern
- Taking an active role in ensuring that appropriate methods of conservation and restoration are used
- Encouraging the responsible ownership, conservation and restoration of ruined structures, and other buildings at risk, in the belief that, in many cases, restoration offers the best means of ensuring their long-term survival
- Promoting the academic study of Scottish castles, of the circumstances which gave rise to their creation, and of all the people and activities associated with them
- Building up knowledge and skills databases for use by all members
- Providing advice on repair and restoration
- Bringing together potential restorers with appropriate properties for restoration
- Liaising with other bodies, including government departments, local authorities and other conservation organisations, in the pursuit of the above objectives
- Organising national and international meetings in the context of the above objectives

Membership

Membership is available to all, and enquiries should be directed to:

Stuart Morris of Balgonie yr
Balgonie Castle
By Markinch
Fife
KY7 6HQ

Activities

- Organised visits throughout Scotland and abroad to both ruined and occupied properties not normally open to the public
- Annual Conference

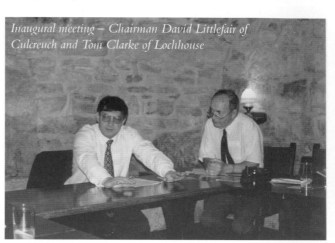

Inaugural meeting – Chairman David Littlefair of Culcreuch and Tom Clarke of Lochhouse

Useful Addresses

HISTORIC SCOTLAND
Longmore House
Salisbury Place
Edinburgh
Tel: 0131 668 8600

NATIONAL TRUST FOR SCOTLAND
5 Charlotte Square
Edinburgh
Tel: 0131 226 5922

**ROYAL COMMISSION ON THE AN-
CIENT AND HISTORICAL MONU-
MENTS OF SCOTLAND**
John Sinclair House
16 Bernard Terrace
Edinburgh
Tel: 0131 662 1456

SCOTTISH NATIONAL HERITAGE
46 Crossgates
Cupar, Fife
KY15 5HS
Tel: 01334 654038

WOODLAND TRUST
Glenruthven Mill
Abbey Road
Auchterarder
PH3 1DP

SCOTTISH WILDLIFE TRUST
Cramond House
Kirk Cramond
Cramond Glebe Road
Edinburgh
EH4 6NS
Tel: 0131 312 7765

FORESTRY COMMISSION
Perth Conservancy
10 York Place
Perth
PH2 8EP
Tel: 01738 442830

South Scotland Forest Enterprise
55/57 Moffat Road
Dumfries
DG1 1NP
Tel: 01387 269171

Further Reading

The Castellated & Domestic Architecture of Scotland. (5 vols).
Macgibbon & Ross. The definitive work.

The Kingdom of Fife: an Illustrated Architectural Guide. (G. L. Pride).

Castles of Fife: A Heritage Guide.
Fife Regional Council.

Discovering Scottish Castles.
(M. Salter). A gazetteer of 1026 castles.

The Castles of Scotland: comprehensive reference and gazetteer to more than 2000 castles. **Second edn.**
(M. Coventry).

The Fortified House in Scotland.
(5 vols). (N. Tranter)

The Castles of Scotland.
(5 vols). (M. Salter)